THE A-Z OF 100 POPULAR COLLECTABLES

THE A-Z OF 100 POPULAR COLLECTABLES

Nick Fletcher

WARD LOCK LIMITED · LONDON

This book is for Jenny and Malcolm,
always there when I need them.

First published in Great Britain in 1986
by Ward Lock Limited, 8 Clifford Street
London W1X 1RB, an Egmont Company

Photography by Mitch Jenkins

Text set in Gill Sans Light and Goudy Old Style
by MS Filmsetting Limited, Frome, Somerset

Printed and bound in Spain by Graficas Reunidas

British Library Cataloguing in Publication Data
Fletcher, Nick
    The A–Z of 100 popular collectables.
    1. Antiques
    1. Title
    745.1   NK1125
ISBN 0-7063-6466-X

ACKNOWLEDGMENTS

For the loan of some of the items photographed, the author
and publishers are indebted to:

John and Margaret Hamore, Mike and Shirley Justice, Mr
and Mrs G.W. Selby, Ken and Glenys Beale, John and
Maureen Clifton, Judith, Christabell and Cassie Haley, Alan
Sherratt and Mrs Prudence Sherratt, Stuart and Sandra
Rutter and John and Kate Rutter of Doghouse Antiques,
Walsall, Staffordshire, Neil Bonner, John Clifford, Richard
Deakin, Ian Tavernor, Chris Ecclestone, Angela Brown, Ray
Heath, Alan Burman, Frank Wakelam, Jenny Fletcher,
Malcolm Rocke, and Peter and Diane Cooksley of
Kingsthorpe Antiques, Northamptonshire.

Special thanks to Pam Cardwell for locating additional
research material.

Contents

Part I

INTRODUCTION

WHAT IS AN ANTIQUE?

Until just a few years ago, collecting antiques was largely confined to the wealthy, but now, thanks to a plethora of books on antiques, as well as magazines, newspaper articles and television programmes, the collecting craze has spread rapidly.

This tremendous interest in items from the past has meant that to some extent the word 'antique' has had to be redefined. To the purist, anything made after 1830 is not considered to be an antique. The reason for this is that around that date a certain amount of mechanization was introduced into manufacturing and this could often mean an inevitable decline in quality. For instance, until that time furniture had been hand-made, but when machinery was invented that could turn chair legs and reproduce carving, then purists consider that the great age of craftsmanship was over. However, if antique dealers had to stock their shops with items made before 1830, most of them would be out of business within a week. Today, enough of our antiques from this period have been exported or gone into private collections or museums, that very little from the golden age of antiques is left on the open market.

These days the word 'antique' is defined rather more loosely and I think most dealers would consider the term applies to items made before about 1910, the end of the Edwardian era. However, if dealers had to confine their stocks to goods made prior to this date, they would still be in difficulty because demand far outstrips supply. Thus for many dealers the terms 'antiques' and 'collectables' have become interchangeable. Collectables now embrace items made as recently as the 1960s – as evidenced by the sales of rock and roll memorabilia held by great auction houses such as Sotheby's and Christie's.

This new fascination with yesteryear has succeeded in opening up the floodgates and created a pastime in which almost everyone can indulge.

Collectables can cost as little as fifty pence, so you no longer have to be wealthy to become a collector, but before you set out to join the new legions of collectors it is as well to know something about how antiques dealers conduct their business. When you understand how they operate, you will be well prepared to play them at their own game, to hunt out bargains, and to get good value for money.

HOW THE TRADE WORKS

There are those who believe that antiques traders don't really work, that dealing is a lazy life with rich pickings. The truth is very different. Today the antiques trade is a highly overcrowded profession. Recent high unemployment has created a greater trend towards self-employment. As a result the antiques trade has attracted a large influx of newcomers, many professional and many more part-time. Such competitiveness inevitably forces prices upwards as more and more dealers compete for a limited number of antiques and collectables.

In conducting their business, dealers have to travel long distances in their search for stock and they often have to work very unsocial hours. They must also be prepared to suffer seasonal declines in trade as a fickle public turns its attention to more important concerns such as holidays. It is a fact that the public is such an unreliable source of custom that the vast majority of antiques and collectables are brought and sold between dealers. This aspect of the trade is often puzzling to an outsider, who wonders how dealers can keep buying and selling among themselves and still make a living. The answer is simple enough – almost all antiques come on to the open market at too low a price. The true value of an item is reached only when it finds a home with a collector and its journey to that home can involve it passing through the hands of a number of dealers, all of whom earn a small amount from it as it passes by. Let me give you a hypothetical but typical example of how this works.

Dealer A has a shop in a small provincial town. A lady comes into the shop with an ornate silver bowl which she says has been in the family for many years. The dealer is not a specialist in silver, but he can see that it is a pleasant example of its kind and while not knowing its true worth, buys it from her at an agreed price which he expects will leave him some profit. Next day, dealer B calls at the shop. He is from a larger town thirty miles away and makes regular runs into the country, calling at shops to see what he can find. His knowledge of silver is a little more specialized than dealer A and he realizes that he can sell the bowl at a higher price in his shop, so he gives the dealer A a small profit and takes the bowl with him.

Dealer B puts the bowl on sale at his shop for a higher price and a few days later is visited by dealer C, who has a shop in London. Because of the influx of foreign buyers in London, prices tend to be higher there so dealer C knows that he can sell the bowl for a greater amount at his shop, and buys it.

But the journey of the silver bowl may not end there. It could change hands two or three times among London dealers, each of whom feel that they have potential custom for it at ever increasing prices. It is likely that a visiting Dutch, German or American dealer may purchase the bowl, take it to their home country and put it on sale there. Again, the bowl could change hands among several foreign dealers, eventually being bought by a private collector at a price many times greater than when it started out on its journey.

Along the way a number of dealers have earned a small profit from the bowl and there is nothing wrong in this; it does not mean that the private collector at the end of the chain has not obtained value for his money. It is not antiques dealers who ultimately determine the price for

items, but the eventual purchasers. The collector who buys this silver bowl will feel *he* has received value for money and that it was worth the amount he paid.

Of course, not all items go on such long journeys. Some may only change hands once or twice. This system is just one factor among a number which explain why antiques can vary so widely in price. It can depend entirely on which stage of its journey you chance across it.

Another reason for price fluctuation is the circumstances in which dealers acquire their stock. Wherever possible, they like to buy from private sources – in other words the homes of the general public – because they feel there is a greater chance of acquiring the item at far less than its potential value. This does not necessarily mean that all dealers set out to trick the public when buying from them. Most dealers are quite prepared to pay a fair price of around two-thirds of what they expect to sell it for. They prefer to buy from the public because it removes the competitive edge which often forces prices upwards when traders compete against each other – at auctions, for instance.

Dealers replenish their stock by keeping a close eye on the 'for sale' columns in their local newspapers, by advertising themselves and claiming they pay top prices, and from other sources such as calling at antique shops, antique centres and antiques fairs. In short, dealers get their stock from all the places the public can buy from. With just a little knowledge you can quickly make the best of this situation.

HOW TO BUY

I am often asked to give advice on buying tactics, as if the purchase of, for example, a copper kettle is a military-style operation in a war that exists between antiques dealer and customer. Clearly, a dealer is out to get as much as he can for an item and the customer wants to acquire it for the smallest possible amount, so to this extent a battle of wits often does exist.

I have often been told off, sometimes with very short words, by antiques dealers who feel it is wrong for me to give any helpful advice to the public on how to buy antiques, but I have no hesitation in doing so because I believe that the more the public knows, the more interest and confidence there will be on the part of the customer. This is also healthy for the trade as a whole. Customers who are afraid of an antiques dealer might feel some mystique surrounds him and his business and are likely to view the buying of antiques as something of an ordeal and therefore to engage in it as infrequently as possible. If the public could be as comfortable about buying antiques as they are about buying groceries from a supermarket, it is likely the antiques trade would substantially increase the volume of its business.

Whether you intend buying at a shop, an antiques centre, a fair or an auction, you are still likely to come into direct contact with an antiques dealer and there are a number of essential rules which I feel help to even up this often one-sided confrontation.

There are those who think it important not to display any outward sign of wealth when you visit an antiques dealer. They feel that if you pull up outside his shop in your new Jaguar and step out in an expensive suit or a mink stole, the dealers who do not visibly price their stock may well make upward mental adjustments as you walk through the door. Such customers therefore think that it is best to arrive in something like an elderly Morris 1000 or perhaps better still, by bicycle, and that it is best to wear something dowdy, crumpled and, if possible, threadbare.

They also take the view that once inside the shop, they should chat to the dealer, making sure they mention they have been recently made redundant or have a widowed mother to support. They obviously feel that by trying to establish a rather impoverished image, they are likely to pull a fast one on the dealer and be in a more favourable position to gain price reductions. This sort of attitude is not to be encouraged. While I am sure there will be a tiny minority of dealers who do adjust the price to suit the customer's apparent means, the vast majority trade very fairly and honestly and there is no need for customers to embark upon elaborate ruses.

However, agreeing on a price is an important matter for both parties and these days haggling over the price of antiques is so widespread that to try to disguise that fact would be churlish. Dealers operate a special discount system among themselves, usually about 10 percent off the marked price. Clearly, if they are prepared to sell the item to another dealer for 10 percent less, they really are prepared to sell it to *you* for the same amount. It is unwise however, to claim that you are in the trade yourself, for the dealer can soon rumble you by asking about your shop, what you specialize in and what you think of the latest auction trends. It is far better, on finding an item you want to buy, to set about some straightforward haggling, and there are several ways to go about this.

The first is simply to ask what the 'best price' is. This is a semi-trade term and will usually result in a few pounds being knocked off the price. If, however, the dealer is resistant to reducing the price, I consider it fair in this battle of wits to employ more subtle methods. One is to look longingly and lingeringly at the item in question, enthuse over it and then put it down with a regretful look. Start moving hesitantly towards the door, audibly murmuring, 'I really love that, but it's just a little more than I can afford.' The dealer, seeing a possible sale slipping away, may well call you back, saying he may, after all, be able to help you out slightly with the price.

There are a number of variations on this theme. You can say you have a budget of a certain amount to spend on a present for a friend and you can't exceed that budget. This often results in the price of the item in question being lowered to exactly the budget amount.

These more subtle methods are much more likely to achieve results than the rather abrasive approach which can upset dealers. It is not a good idea to look at an item marked at, say £50 and say rather brusquely, 'I'll give you £25'. Even allowing for the trade's roguish reputation, a dealer will very rarely be making a 100 percent or even 50 percent profit. As best you can hope for the price being reduced by 10 to 20 percent at the most, but every little helps.

There are collectors who use much more devious tactics in a bid to get the price of antiques reduced. For instance, they might take children into the shop with them. A couple of small children, if noisy and energetic and prone to race around, can strike terror into the heart of a dealer. If they are also dripping ice cream onto the furniture and smearing chocolate onto the upholstery, then dealers begin to develop instant ulcers. I have known some hastily reduce prices simply in order to get the family out of the shop as quickly as possible. Large dogs with wagging tails can sometimes have a similar effect.

Such intimidatory methods are to be deplored, as it is in everyone's interest for the relationship between customer and dealer to be harmonious rather than antagonistic. Dealers can, if allowed, be very friendly and helpful people, but they can be quickly upset and irritated by rude, over-demanding customers. It is more preferable to clinch a deal with a smile rather than a frown, and customers and dealers should bear this in mind at all times.

WHERE TO BUY

As I suggested earlier, you have the opportunity to buy at all the sources used by the antiques trade itself. However, you should remember that an antiques dealer does provide a service. By buying from him, you save yourself the trouble and expense of locating the item, cleaning it and possibly repairing it. To buy direct from source you may have to involve yourself in all those aspects.

You can, of course, peruse the miscellaneous sales columns in your local newspapers for the type of items you want and then hotfoot it to the seller to see if you can strike a bargain – but you'll have to be fast. The sharpest antique dealers get the first edition and are likely to be on the doorstep with pound notes in their hand almost before the ink is dry on the newspaper. If you do beat them to it, then you face the same problems they face. Public awareness of the value of antiques is so great these days, thanks to TV programmes such as the *Antiques Roadshow* and other publicity, that people often think their items are worth far more than they really are, so you then have the same difficulty as the dealer. You have to talk them down to a realistic level. Another difficulty in following up advertisements is that they are often unintentionally misleading. An advertiser is quite capable of unwittingly describing a table as Georgian, only to mean George VI. You can involve yourself in a

lot of wasted time and effort and so many people do prefer to leave such tedious work to the dealers.

Auctions, shops, antiques fairs and antiques centres are all dealt with individually, but I am often asked if there is any advantage in buying from one rather than another. Auctions do have the edge, since by buying at auction you do avoid paying the dealer's profit which is already included in the price at shops, fairs and centres. But auctions do have their disadvantages, as we shall see.

BUYING AT AUCTION

Auctions are an excellent place to buy for genuine bargains can be found there. Many people, however, find being at a saleroom a nightmare experience, and something to be feared. Yet there is no need to worry whatsoever about buying at auction, providing you understand the way they operate.

Auction lots are made up of items from both private individuals and from antiques dealers. Unless you have inside knowledge, there is no way of knowing which lots are from private sources and which are from the trade. However, this need not be important as it doesn't affect your assessment of what you are prepared to pay for a particular item once the bidding starts.

Before you begin bidding, you should make a point of attending what is called the 'viewing'. This will be held and advertised some days before the sale and there is often also a viewing period on the morning of the sale itself. It is vital that you examine any items you may consider buying, for if you buy blind, only to find a vase is cracked or a chair is riddled with woodworm, you have no form of redress. Auction law says, in effect, let the buyer beware. You have a duty to satisfy yourself as to the age, condition and authenticity of any lot in the auction and to make your own assessment of it.

Although the auctioneers read out a description of each lot, they are not bound by it, nor is the vendor. Errors do creep in, for all descriptions are simply a matter of opinion. Often in smaller, provincial salerooms the auctioneers may accept word for word in good faith the description supplied by the vendor, who may be anything but an expert. The only redress you would have in the event of being dissatisfied with a purchase would be if you could show that the auctioneer's or vendor's description was reckless and that is very, very difficult to prove.

Auctions can be exciting events particularly when you are not used to attending them in which case there is often a temptation to get carried away during the bidding. It is very important to decide in advance a limit to the amount you are prepared to pay for a particular item and to stick to that limit. This is precisely the way dealers operate and it is a very professional method of doing business.

People often say that you can't take on the dealers at auction. This is nonsense. Dealers decide in advance how much they are likely to be able to sell a particular lot for and will bid only up to a particular percentage of that amount. Once their buying price is exceeded, they lose interest and wait for the next lot. You have to remember that dealers do not normally take the buying of lots as some sort of personal crusade. While *you* may have noted down only one or two items to buy, *they* may have noted dozens. They don't expect to buy them all and are, therefore, resistant to getting carried away on a wave of enthusiasm.

If a dealer estimates he can sell an item for £100, he is unlikely to bid more than about £70 for it in auction. If you, then, outbid the dealer by another £5, you are not paying too much for the item, but merely saving yourself the difference between the auction price and the price the dealer would have retailed the item for in his shop.

It follows that buying in auction can save you between 20 and 30 percent, but this only works successfully if you do have some knowledge of the current market price of the item concerned and are aware that the dealers have dropped out of the bidding. It is easy to find yourself in a situation where you are frantically bidding against other private individuals, all of whom have thrown caution to the wind, with the result that the item ends up at far more than you would ever have to pay for it in an antiques shop.

If you attend an auction room regularly, you will quickly get to know who the dealers are. They are the ones that tend to huddle together and never look very happy! They can also be identified by the auctioneer calling out their name regularly, though he may know them so well he doesn't bother to.

Frequently at auctions you will see the porters holding up an item which will appear to be wonderful, yet attract very low bidding. There is an immediate temptation to put your hand in the air and snap up this apparent bargain. Beware. The chances are you haven't viewed this item and the reason why the bidding is so low is that it has some major defect. It may be riddled with woodworm, badly damaged, or have some components missing. If you are prepared to take the chance, well and good. Occasionally something has been overlooked at the viewing. It may have been tucked away out of sight or surrounded by other items and difficult to get at. In such instances you can end up with a bargain, but realistically, the chances are that you will end up either with a piece of furniture that has so much woodworm it could walk around on its own, or a piece of porcelain that has been reconstructed from so many shattered pieces that it becomes a tribute to the glue industry.

I am frequently asked if dealers form 'rings' at auctions in an effort to keep prices low. The answer is yes. Such rings can be a common occurrence in some parts of the country, particularly the more rural areas. While illegal, they are very difficult to prove in court, and there have been only a couple of convictions in recent years.

A ring operates when a number of dealers get together before an auction and agree not to bid against each other. They usually appoint one dealer to bid on behalf of them all. This, of course, reduces the competition and keeps prices lower than they would otherwise be. After the sale, the dealers take the goods elsewhere, and hold a private mini-sale among themselves, saving large sums of money compared with what they would have had to pay at open auction.

Some members of a ring may not want any of the 'booty' and are paid a sum in cash by other members for having kept out of the bidding. I know of one dealer who earns a substantial part of his income by turning up at sales with no intention of buying. He merely wants to draw his 'wages'.

In 1983, in one of the rare cases to come to court, nine antiques dealers from Shropshire and Wales were each fined £500, with £300 costs, after admitting agreeing not to bid against each other at an auction near Aberystwyth. The ruse was uncovered when a police officer saw a procession of heavily-laden estate cars heading for a deserted beach. He followed and witnessed the group of dealers re-auctioning among themselves valuable antiques they had bought cheaply at a country house sale earlier that day. One dealer had openly boasted that a carpet he had bought for on £720 could be sold for more than £3,000. This shows how seriously dealers can keep down auction prices when they conspire.

Happily, major rings are few and far between, but at almost every auction sale one or two dealers who are friends will almost certainly agree not to bid against each other on certain items. Such an agreement is illegal, but almost impossible to prove.

BUYING FROM SHOPS

There are two types of antique shops: up-market shops and a wide variety of general shops. Fortunately, it is easy to tell which is which, and thus decide what you are likely to get for your money.

Up-market shops look very posh – the word 'antiques' above the window has been painted in gothic lettering by a professional signwriter; the brass handle on the door is polished daily. In the window you are likely to see a few carefully selected items: an early oak lowboy, a carved chair, a highly polished table upon which there might sit a blue and white pot of oriental origin. There will be no sign of any price tags.

Often such shops are found in tourist areas, sometimes in converted Georgian buildings, old barns, or renovated cottages with thatched roof and leaded windows. Such shops frequently advertise in glossy antiques magazines; often their advertisement will show just one fine piece of furniture. Again, no price will be mentioned. You have to realize that at this kind of shop you are likely to be getting authentic antiques of the highest quality. You will also be paying every penny of the full market price for them, and are

unlikely to find a bargain at this sort of establishment.

It is not uncommon for such shops to be manned, not by the proprietor, but by an aged lady sitting in a dark corner knitting or by an au pair girl who speaks fractured English and has to look up the prices in a book. There are those who think that in such circumstances, the owner is probably wintering in the Bahamas on the hefty profit he has made in the preceding months. There is sometimes a grain of truth in this theory, but on the whole it is an uncharitable view. The owner is far more likely to be out of the area acquiring more stock.

Posh shops also feel it is somewhat beneath them to actually put a price ticket on anything. If a ticket is present, it is likely to show an unintelligible code. This does not denote the selling price, but merely the price the dealer paid when the item was brought in. It reminds him what the piece cost and allows him to judge what he thinks you are capable of paying for it. Any form of haggling at this kind of shop is normally frowned upon. The owners are often elderly, quite wealthy, and do not need to turn over stock quickly.

If the owner is present, there are those who think that you can tell a great deal about him or her from their appearance. Some collectors I know are reluctant to buy from dealers who wear lots of jewellery, or sport a suntan. They feel it is they, the customers, who are paying for the gold from Cartier and the holiday in St Tropez. This is a rather cynical view, as dealers are just as entitled to jewellery and holidays as any other trader. If a butcher or a grocer appears wealthy, no-one really gives it a second thought.

Downmarket from these heady antique shops are all the rest, ranging from back-street second-hand dealers to retired colonels boosting their pensions running small antique shops in country villages. There is an even chance of a bargain at any of these establishments. They normally work on a smaller profit margin and a quicker turn-over of stock than more up-market premises.

If you are touring round looking for a bargain in the antique shops, then look out for the sort of sign you'll find half hidden in a hedge down a remote country lane. The word 'antiques' will appear to have been painted most unprofessionally. The paint will have run badly on all the letters and you might even find the word 'antiques' mis-spelled. This type of sign, particularly prevalent in Wales, usually denotes a part-time country dealer of very limited means. His stock will consist of the left-overs from local auctions, items he has found on rubbish tips, or begged from friends and neighbours. His knowledge is likely to be limited and he will often be incapable of recognising a rare and valuable item. So it is possible, once in a while, if you have adequate knowledge, to ferret around among the junk and bric-a-brac that threatens to overrun his shop or home and emerge triumphant with a valuable piece of art nouveau, a top quality water colour or a first-class piece of porcelain at a mere fraction of its true worth.

BUYING AT ANTIQUES FAIRS

The antiques fair is a fairly modern phenomenon and has burgeoned greatly in recent years, largely due to the vast number of part-time dealers who require an outlet for their wares. At town halls and village halls all over the country each weekend of the year you can find a choice of antiques fairs advertised in the local press. Some are high-quality events with goods having to conform to a dateline i.e., where only goods made before a specified date are on sale; others are little more than fleamarkets where LP records, electric shavers and paperback books can be found alongside Victorian vases and Edwardian furniture.

The particular benefit of buying at antiques fairs is that prices tend to be quite competitive. With so many dealers under one roof, there is a slight levelling down of prices and this can only be good for the customer. Dealers who use antiques fairs as an outlet also benefit from lower overheads and this, too, can be reflected in lower prices.

Fairs are usually staged by a promoter who is often an antiques dealer himself. He will hire a public hall, then sub-let sections of it to other dealers for a small charge. His income from this rental and the admission charge to the event enables him to pay for the hall and the advertising involved in promoting the fair, and if the event is well supported, he is likely to emerge from it with a profit. The participating dealers just have their stall rental and travelling expenses to take into account.

Many dealers operate entirely by working the antiques fairs and do not have a shop as a base. Most fairs will see around fifty dealers taking part, but there can be events which run to several hundred dealers. Fairs can be very useful if you are looking for a particular item, perhaps for a present, for they save you an endless tracking around individual shops. With so many goods under one roof you are almost certain to find what you are looking for and then you can start bargaining. Haggling over price is very much a part of the informal atmosphere of an antiques fair and dealers do expect their asking prices to be challenged.

That elusive bargain that everyone seems to want in the world of antiques can often be found at antiques fairs. Part-time dealers with slender knowledge can often unwittingly display quite rare items which can be snapped up by you if you are lucky, by other dealers if you are not.

While the advantages of buying at antiques fairs are quite apparent, I am often asked if there are any disadvantages. There is just one. If you buy something from a fair and have reason to be dissatisfied with it, or wish to contact the dealer about it for some other reason, you may have difficulty getting in touch with him. He is unlikely to live locally, as dealers travel considerable distances to trade at antiques fairs. Most people don't bother to note down the name and address of a dealer they buy from at a fair.

On the whole, the advent of antiques fairs has done the trade a lot of good and provided a tremendous boost to business. Fairs have made antiques and collectables more widely available to many people and have made a very large contribution to the growth of collecting in recent years.

BUYING AT ANTIQUES CENTRES

Antiques centres, like fairs, offer a vast choice of goods under one roof, and do save a good deal of shoe leather. Centres are also a fairly recent innovation forced on dealers by the ever-rising overheads of high street or even suburban shops.

Centres work by dealers getting together and renting space or even entire rooms in suitably large buildings, thus creating a number of mini-shops in a compact venue. The rent, rates, heating, lighting and advertising for the centre are in effect shared by all the participating dealers who each pay an agreed amount every week, depending on the size of their unit.

While such centres are usually populated by professional dealers, they are also used by the more active part-time dealers who are not able to run their own shop, but whose stock is sufficient to justify a unit at an antiques centre. The chief attraction of an antiques centre to a part-time dealer is that because the centres are run by a manager, who is often one of the dealers, there is no need for the unit to be continuously manned. The management usually charge dealers a handling or administration fee of 5 percent of the price of each item sold.

Antiques centres offer the same possibility of bargains as antiques fairs and have no real drawbacks. The number of centres is growing fast and is likely to continue as increasing overheads force more dealers to abandon shops and seek a more low cost outlet.

THE PROTECTION OF THE LAW

I was once involved in a very heated argument with a dealer over whether a pair of Victorian pictures were water colours or prints. It was an important point to settle, as there would have been a price difference of about £50. He insisted they were water colours, whereas I felt there was real doubt about the matter, and felt they were prints. He took the view that whether or not they were water colours was unimportant, because in the event of him being wrong, there could be no comeback from a customer because he himself *believed* that they were water colours.

Such an attitude is not uncommon in the antiques trade, as most dealers think that any description they apply is merely an opinion and because of that, it protects them from any later claim should the authenticity of the item come into dispute. But in law they are NOT protected from applying a false description, merely because

they give an opinion in good faith.

Contrary to popular belief, there are a number of laws which relate to the sale of antiques. For instance law relating to a verbal or written contract made between buyer and seller applies, and even a quite recent Act of Parliament, the 1979 Sale of Goods Act, brings antiques within its scope. This Act states that in the case of a sale by a trader, it is an implied condition of the contract that the goods are of merchantable quality and fit for their purpose. In the case of new goods this is quite easy to determine, but in the case of secondhand or antique goods the question of merchantable quality will clearly depend upon the exact nature of the contract. In some cases antique goods may be quite badly damaged, but still of acceptable quality because of the nature of the article. Antiques may also be severely worn or no longer fit for their original purpose, yet still acceptable, but it is still possible for a customer to claim against an antiques dealer under the Sale of Goods Act, depending on the circumstances of the contract between the two parties.

Buyers of antiques are also protected by the Misrepresentation Act of 1967. This Act makes it clear that anyone selling antiques, and who falsely describes the goods, can be sued for a refund or for compensation. 'It does not matter whether or not the misrepresentation was made innocently or fraudulently,' a senior Trading Standards Officer told me. 'The buyer will still be entitled to compensation, even though the seller believed that the description he applied to the goods was correct.'

If no description or statements are made about the goods, then the buyer must make up his own mind about them, and will not be entitled to compensation if he makes a wrong assumption.

In addition to the law relating to the sale and descriptions of antiques, the 1968 Trades Descriptions Act also applies. This act makes it a criminal offence for anyone to apply a false description to any goods and the seller can be prosecuted for applying that false description. 'Once again, it does not matter whether or not the seller knew that the description was false,' said the Trading Standards Officer. 'Antiques sellers should be fully aware of this situation, since it is likely that many descriptions of goods will be made in the course of their business. Indeed, the very word "antique" may constitute a description and in some cases may be false,' he said.

It is also worth noting that dealers cannot negate descriptions they apply to goods by having a disclaimer notice on display or in a catalogue. For instance, if the seller is describing a piece of furniture as seventeenth century, but has a notice on display saying that he cannot be held responsible for any description made, then in law such a notice will have no effect.

If you do buy something and later have cause to doubt its authenticity, your first step should be to return it to the dealer in question and raise the matter with him. In most cases you will find the dealer only too willing to try to remedy the situation. There may well have been some misunderstanding or lack of communication relating to the sale of the item to you, or he may have sold it in good faith, believing it to be what he said it was. If you are able to show him that his description was wrong, he should be only too willing to take the item back and give you a full refund. It is only if he is reluctant to do this, or totally refuses, that you should consider reporting the matter to your local Trading Standards Office.

It is a wise move to insist on a written receipt from the dealer when you buy an item. Ask not only for a brief description of the item, but also an estimate of its age and make sure that he signs the receipt. Any honest dealer will have no hesitation in giving such a receipt. If a dealer refuses, it means either he has no confidence in his own judgement, or that he has some knowledge or suspicion of the item in question and does not want to commit himself in writing. In such circumstances it is clearly unwise to complete the transaction.

FAKES

The combination of increasing demand and limited supply has resulted in a new growth industry within the world of antiques, that of faking. Perhaps at this point I should stress the main difference between a fake and a reproduction. A true reproduction is a copy and it pretends to be nothing more. A fake is an item which has been aged, altered or disguised with the intention of passing it off as the genuine article.

Faking is a deplorable practice, but one which is increasingly widespread and helps give the antiques trade a bad name. Unfortunately, unscrupulous men exist in all businesses and are beyond the control of the honest majority. Few areas of antiques are safe from the dubious art of the faker.

Metalware, for example, is extremely easy to age overnight. The use of acids and chemicals can transform a new piece of brass or copper into something that looks as if it hasn't seen the light of day for centuries. Warming pans, tankards, swords and kettles are commonly aged with the intention of fooling the buyer. Some of these fakes are so authentic-looking that they dupe even experienced dealers, who then go on to sell them in good faith. But there are, of course, many dealers who are aware of the racket and merely take advantage of it. Even some of London's top auction houses have been fooled.

The forger's art is not just confined to metalware. He can quickly turn his attention to pottery and porcelain which can be baked in high temperature ovens to produce glaze cracks. The items can then be immersed in tea to put a hundred years of staining into those cracks overnight. The bases of vases and figures can be filed and rubbed on concrete to produce the natural wear which would take years to occur.

Once fakes are filtered onto the antiques circuit, changing hands several times, often in good faith, among dealers and through auction rooms, it can be very difficult to detect them. Often, fakes are not made in Britain, but as far away as Taiwan. From there I have seen replicas of Victorian cast iron mechanical money boxes which are available ready rusted after being buried in damp conditions. Genuine examples of these money boxes can fetch several hundred pounds. This kind of situation adds weight to my recommendation that you always obtain a detailed signed receipt whenever you purchase antiques. It may not in itself prevent you buying a fake, but it will certainly enable you to seek compensation if the authenticity is put in doubt at a later stage.

Furniture is the main target for the faker. Wood is an easily workable material and the wear of centuries can be put on in a matter of minutes by a skilled craftsman, who should be using his talents for a more legitimate purpose. I have known the damaged front legs of a seventeenth-century dresser be replaced by ones made from an old farm gatepost. The result was virtually undetectable, even to the experienced eye, and the dresser went on to be sold as 'completely original' for a large sum of money. I have seen Victorian and Edwardian wardrobes dismantled, cut up and re-assembled into 'absolutely genuine' corner cupboards and display cabinets.

Deliberate maltreatment of a newly-made piece of furniture is known as 'distressing'. It is done by causing severe abrasion using chains, files or other tools, or by blows from a hammer. The intention is to duplicate the wear and tear of a century or more of daily use, and such distressing is often only detectable because it has been overdone. The faker tends to exaggerate the wear to make sure that it is noticed and they sometimes use a spokeshave to create wear on a part of the furniture which would not normally be the subject of heavy wear, for example the back stretchers of chairs.

There are any number of ways of distressing a piece of furniture by bruising, scraping, scratching, gouging or even beating. In all these cases, detection can often be a simple matter of good observation. One of the most certain methods of detecting a fake is to look for signs of staining — not the staining of the immediately visible surfaces, but the inaccessible underpart of the piece concerned, for instance the underside of a chair or table, drawer linings, or the insides or backs of cupboards. A genuine eighteenth century or earlier piece of furniture should show no sign of stain whatsoever. Discoloration by age or dirt will be visible, but it will be on bare wood.

Reproductions or copies must of necessity be artificially coloured by staining, to impart the desired impression of age. It is important to remember that antiques were originally sold as new items, therefore efforts to achieve a bogus aged appearance were completely unnecessary.

Stain is also used, often rather crudely, on frontal and visible surfaces. Applied thickly, it is allowed to half dry, at which stage patches are wiped off to expose near bare wood in places where signs of wear would be expected. Highlights of carved and turned ornament, chair rails and arms and front edges of cupboards, are obvious places for this treatment. This method of age simulation was particularly common in the early years of this century and is still in use today.

There is no way a book can teach you how to tell a fake from the authentic item. All that I can hope to do is to point you in the right direction and hope that your own observations and common sense will do the rest. Only by examining furniture over a period of time can you readily distinguish the subtle differences which can lead you to expose a fake. If you do want to learn about furniture, then examine as much of it as you can; that way you learn to recognize quality and authenticity.

One useful pointer is to examine the patina of a piece of furniture. The patina refers to the distinctive glossy surface texture built up on the wood over a period of many years. The depth and general appearance of true patina can be achieved only gradually and naturally with wear, usage, slight atmospheric erosion, waxing and polishing. It is therefore difficult for the faker to duplicate and usually a surface which has been given a rapid and recent gloss will stand out like a sore thumb once you are familiar with what true patina really looks like.

Another way of trying to detect fake furniture is to pay attention to the weight of the article. In the case of an eighteenth-century chair, for example, it would most likely be made of Cuban mahogany. A nineteenth-century copy, or even a twentieth-century copy, would weigh much less as a lighter mahogany or baywood from Honduras would probably be used.

Carved embellishments should also be examined carefully on furniture. As a general rule, eighteenth-century carving is deeper and crisper than later work. Victorian craftsmen took less trouble and the result is shallow, almost careless carving.

Colour, too, is important in assessing wood, particularly mahogany. Reddish or orange mahogany is almost certainly Victorian, as earlier mahogany was much darker.

If you make a detailed study of furniture, you

will find there are many other pointers too. Early veneers, for instance, were thicker and hand-cut. Later veneers were machine-cut and almost paper thin. The direction the grain runs, the way drawers are dovetailed and the use of beading or moulding can all help pinpoint precisely when a piece was made. Even screws are important. Until about 1850 screws did not taper to a point and the slot was hand-cut and rarely ever central.

Such tiny clues, when linked to keen observation, can lead to fakes being exposed. But there are, sadly, fakers whose knowledge and craftsmanship enable them to turn out almost undetectable items. The experienced antiques dealer has, I feel, a duty to try to protect the public from these forgeries. Unfortunately, there are too many dealers who not only encourage the faker, but actually commission work from him.

In view of the ever-soaring demand for antiques, it is a problem which is unlikely to go away, and all one can do is to be ever alert and take nothing for granted. Buying from old established dealers who are proud of their reputations is one way of minimizing the risk.

BEWARE THE KNOCKER

Polite, charming, often well dressed and well spoken (but then rogues and conmen usually are), thousands of elderly people fall victim to men who arrive at their door with a cheery smile and a handful of cash. They are known as 'knockers', bogus antique dealers who trick old folk into parting with valuables at a fraction of their true worth.

The knockers tend to work a town area by area, with terraced homes a special target as they are usually occupied by the elderly, who are more likely to have antiques and other valuables without realizing how much they are worth.

The ruses these men use vary considerably. Sometimes they claim to be from London, sometimes they claim to be buying on behalf of rich Americans. They claim to pay the highest possible prices for antique furniture, clocks, silver, jewellery and paintings. Often they will use mild intimidation to get into a house, especially if an elderly person is alone. With wads of cash in hand, they offer seemingly generous prices for worthless articles and then having won the occupier's confidence, offer low prices for really valuable items. Then the trickery starts.

They pay for all the low-priced items and take them away, saying they will be back the next day with a van to collect and pay for all the top-priced items. Of course, they never come back, and they have made off with hundreds, sometimes thousands of pounds worth of valuables for which they may have paid as little as £50. I know of one case where an elderly widow was conned into selling a grandfather clock worth about £500 for just £5 after being told by the knockers that it was worthless. 'No-one wants these old clocks, they are too old-fashioned,' she was told.

Sometimes these rogues operate in pairs and once they have pressured their way into a house, they can resort to out and out theft. While one man keeps the householder talking, the other will flit from room to room, filling his pockets with any small valuables he can find. Sometimes the thefts are not discovered until hours later, by which time the knockers are on their way to another town in search of new victims.

Many of these knockers are itinerants with no fixed base. They work the country end to end, county by county, town by town and village by village, making rich pickings along the way. They usually sell the goods they obtain to antique dealers, who mostly buy them in good faith, although sometimes the low prices being asked should alert the dealer.

'The knockers can be very persuasive, very cunning and use every trick in the book to get into a house,' a senior police officer told me. 'I would advise people not to let these men cross their doorstep. If they do get in under some pretext, never leave them alone in a room. If they call at the door and make an offer for anything, I would advise people not to sell, but to get the items properly valued first. These men offer very low prices and the terrible thing is that once someone has sold them something, even for far less than it is worth, there is very little the police can do, as the sale was made willingly, though the men may have used a lot of persuasion. There is also great difficulty tracing the property. These men move from town to town and if we ever catch up with them, they have already sold the item in question at a profit and it is almost impossible to trace it.'

Though some sectors of the antiques trade will happily buy from the knockers, reputable antique dealers despise them. They know all too well that they bring bad publicity to the trade and help to further tarnish its image. No reputable dealer goes around knocking on doors asking if you have anything to sell. He will normally advertise in the local newspaper, or put a card in his window.

SELLING ANTIQUES

Selling antiques is a major headache for many private individuals, who feel they cannot trust the antiques dealer to treat them fairly. People disposing of antiques seldom have much idea of what their true market value is and thus rely on the antiques dealer to make them a fair offer. Most dealers do offer a realistic price, but there are still many who try to beg the item for little or nothing, and try to persuade the seller that the item has no great value. A common reason put forward is that there is 'no demand' for that particular item.

In the course of my work as a writer and broadcaster, I am frequently asked if I can give any advice on how to ensure that any offers dealers make are fair. One method requires you to do a bit of homework. Whether you are selling a large piece of furniture or a small piece of porcelain, it is quite easy to check up on approximate market values. All you have to do is take the time to browse around one or two local antiques shops, visit an antiques fair, or perhaps your local auction rooms. You are bound to come across items which are quite similar to the ones you have for sale and determine what sort of prices are being asked for them.

Obviously, you should not expect to get this full price from an antiques dealer who, after all, has to make a living, but it is reasonable to expect an honest dealer to offer you about two-thirds of his retail price. If, however, the item you are selling is damaged or needs any renovation, you must expect the offer to be somewhat lower, depending on the amount of renovation to be carried out.

If you have a number of items to sell, and don't wish to spend the time checking up on values yourself, you can call in a professional valuer, who will charge a fee for coming to your home and giving you the benefit of his advice. The names and addresses of valuers can be found in the Yellow Pages. Exactly what they will charge will depend on the amount of time they have to spend with you and how far they have had to travel and, of course, the number of items you ask them to value. In the vast majority of cases, the charge is likely to be about £25, assuming there are just a handful of items to value.

Another way of checking whether you are getting a fair offer is to invite several dealers along at different times and then compare all the offers you get. If they are all very similar, then you are likely to have been treated fairly, but if one or two are much higher than the others, then those are the ones to accept.

Of course, there are people who say why sell to the antiques trade at all? Why not try to do it direct? Well, this is an alternative, but it is not one that most people find very convenient. By selling direct, you are actually trying to reach the customers that the antiques dealer himself will be selling to.

In order to do this, you will have to advertise your goods, whether in the local press or in specialist antiques magazines. In addition to the cost of advertising, you will also have to put up with the inconvenience of people calling to look at the items and often saying it's not what they want. If you adopt this method, you will also have to set some sort of price on what you want for the items because you cannot rely on the buyer being able to assess a fair price.

If you are prepared to put up with the drawbacks of selling direct, go ahead by all means, but most people I know who have tried this have found it very unsatisfactory. In trying to save the antique dealer's profit, they have often ended up out of pocket. For the convenience of a dealer calling at the house, making you an offer and removing the items, it is only right to allow him a reasonable profit margin, and as long as you have taken some steps to ensure you have got a fair deal, then selling to the trade is a simple way of disposing of your antiques.

There are people who prefer to sell only by

auction. Competitive bidding at auctions usually ensures that you do get a fair price and the auctioneers will often advise you of the sort of prices they expect particular pieces to achieve, so that you can if you wish set a reserve price on items. However, auctions do have a number of drawbacks. Not all auction rooms hold sales of antiques weekly and if you place items in a sale, you may have to wait for some time before they are actually sold. Even if the salerooms hold a weekly or fortnightly sale, there is still a short delay which may be compounded by having to wait a few days more before the cheque finally reaches you.

Auctioneers, like everyone else, have to earn their living and make a charge for their services. Most auction houses charge around 15 percent commission on the prices achieved in a sale. A number of auctioneers now charge as much as 20 percent, though sometimes the fee is negotiable, particularly if you are selling a large number of items. VAT is also payable on the amount of the auctioneer's commission (but not on the sale price).

If the auctioneers have to fetch the items from your home, then they are likely to make a charge for this. Some auction houses also charge for storage up to the time of the sale and sometimes add a small amount on for insurance, while some salerooms in London and the provinces operate the 'buyer's premium'. This involves the purchaser having to pay an additional percentage, sometimes as much as 10 percent, on top of the price he has bid. This, of course, can restrict to some extent the price he is prepared to pay.

You may find that while auction rooms are an efficient and reliable way of disposing of antiques, by the time you add all the charges together, you may be paying 25 percent or more to the auctioneers. One advantage of selling by auction is that if you have items that are rare or of a specialized collecting nature, then some auction houses, particularly Sotheby's and Christie's, do hold regular sales devoted to specialist themes. Such sales attract collectors not only from all over Britain, but from abroad and the prices achieved can be very much higher than you would expect to get elsewhere.

Finally, I should mention that there are a number of price guide books on the market which illustrate a wide range of antiques and collectables and give some indication of their value. Unfortunately, people tend to take such values far too literally. As the books themselves stress, they are only a guide, not a price list. Items which are similar, but not identical, to those illustrated, may have a lesser value. The condition of an item can also increase or decrease its value. So while price guide books can be very helpful in pointing you in the right direction, they should not be used to give a definitive value.

FURNITURE – A BRIEF HISTORY

Furniture-making was not a specialized trade in England until about 1500. Until then, furniture was crudely made and entirely practical, with no thought whatsoever given to design. But when the influence of the Italian Renaissance was felt in England, then furniture began to be designed rather than simply made. Use was made of inlay, carving and panelling in an effort to make practical pieces of furniture look more attractive.

The period from about 1550 to 1625 embraces the Tudor, Elizabethan and Jacobean eras. After the rule of Oliver Cromwell (1649–60) came the Restoration period of Charles II, followed by periods associated with William and Mary (1688–1702) and Queen Anne (1702–14).

As the seventeenth century drew to a close, the architectural design of homes changed course and there was a trend towards smaller dwellings. This had a great influence on the style of furniture, as there was a much greater demand for smaller items, but which were still visually pleasing and elegant.

For almost 100 years, from 1720, there was what many regard as the golden age of English furniture, the Georgian period. It was around the start of this 'golden age' that mahogany became the most widely used wood for furniture manufacture. There were two reasons. Early furniture had principally been made of oak, which was eventually superseded by walnut. But demand for walnut during the latter half of the seventeenth century was so great that there arose a shortage of the wood throughout Europe, and a substitute was sought. And when, in

1721, an Act of Parliament eased the heavy import duty on mahogany, that wood soon became the mainstay of the furniture trade.

It was in the Georgian era that the work of the designer began to have real meaning. Of course, there had been great designers in the past, but their work was largely confined to the homes of royalty and nobility. The impact of their work was not felt by ordinary people. But it was a very different story for the three great designers whose work dominates the age of mahogany — Chippendale, Hepplewhite and Sheraton. Their work and published designs had immense impact and their furniture found its way into homes all over the country.

Thomas Chippendale was not the greatest furniture designer of this time. Several men were better craftsmen, among them Holland, Shearer and Kent. But Chippendale is remembered more vividly than his rivals for one simple reason. In 1754 he compiled *The Gentleman and Cabinet-maker's Director*, a catalogue of his designs. This was virtually the first trade pattern book and when published, his reputation was assured.

The importance of pattern books was great. Previously, fashionable London designs had taken years to reach provincial centres and rural areas. With a pattern book, fashionable furniture could be made everywhere soon after its innovation.

George Hepplewhite was another great craftsman who began work in London in 1760. Much of his fame came after his death, for his wife published a book of his designs called *The Cabinetmaker and Upholsterer's Guide* and it was this that gave him his great reputation.

Thomas Sheraton is perhaps the oddest of the three great designers of this age. So far as it is known, Sheraton never made one single piece of furniture himself. He was not really a furniture maker — he was a furniture designer. He never had a workshop, but concentrated purely on teaching and writing. The four-part publication of his principal work, *The Cabinetmaker's and Upholsterer's Drawing Book*, made him famous and his style continued to have influence well into the Regency and Victorian periods and there was even an Edwardian revival.

Robert Adam is another illustrious name from this golden age. He inspired the classical revival with furniture noted for impeccable proportions and attention to detail.

The first thirty years of the nineteenth century are known as the Regency period, though the regency of George, Prince of Wales, lasted only from 1811 to 1820. Even over the full three decades there was little advance in furniture design. There was a fad on French Empire style, which itself was a mixture of Roman, Greek and Egyptian influences. There was also a whimsical phase of orientalism, the Prince Regent being a great enthusiast of Chinese style. His enthusiasm was such that he had the famous Brighton pavilion with its mosque-like turrets built. Towards the end of the Regency period there were signs that there was a deterioration in general standards of craftsmanship, largely due to various types of woodworking machinery introduced about this time.

The reign of William IV — six years — was too short to stamp itself on furniture design and there was little progress in the first twenty years that Queen Victoria was on the throne. There was a mishmash of previous styles — pseudo-classical, mock oriental and neo-Gothic — which reached the height of tastelessness and ostentation in 1851, the year of the Great Exhibition. Much Victorian furniture was poorly designed and even more poorly made and only appears to be good quality when comparing it with the even lower standards of twentieth-century manufacturers.

During the closing years of Victoria's reign there was something of a public outcry against sliding standards of craftsmanship and a number of guilds and associations got together to try to make better, more practical furniture. At the head of this movement was a man called William Morris, who began to make hand-made, superior domestic furniture with simplicity of line and an emphasis on durability.

As the turn of the century approached, there was a short-lived move towards art nouveau designs which swept over from France. Broadly speaking, the Victorian era was an age of embellishment rather than innovation, and only two new pieces of furniture really came into use. One was the ottoman, the other the chesterfield. There was, however, a boost for small furniture since it was fashionable to clutter a Victorian room with items such as small occasional tables, workboxes, firescreens, bookstands, plant-stands, and whatnots. When Queen Victoria died in 1901, the nine-year reign of Edward VII followed and coincided with a revival of the clean, simple lines of Sheraton designs, with widespread use of inlay. Really, that was the last true period for antique furniture, as quality and design fell victim to the increasing need for mass manufacture.

Between the wars oak furniture was in vogue, particularly of the type with barleytwist legs and simple carving. There is an avid market for this rather humble furniture today, as it exudes an honesty and solid, lasting quality which is missing from modern chipboard and plastic offerings.

POTTERY – A BRIEF HISTORY

The first essential for any aspiring collector is to be able to tell the difference between pottery and porcelain. The chief observable difference is that pottery is an opaque earthernware, while porcelain has a translucent quality

The history of pottery-making covers thousands of years from origins in China and Egypt. In Britain the pottery story really starts with the introduction of delftware which came to England with Flemish refugees around 1565 and was produced at Norwich and later Lambeth and Southwark in London, and in Bristol and Liverpool.

The big leap forward in the English pottery manufacturing industry came in the 1740s when creamware was perfected. It was more attractive than delftware and quickly replaced it, becoming the standard body for ordinary domestic wares. Around this time a multiple moulding process was also discovered which made the mass manufacture of pottery much easier. The most famous name in English pottery is Josiah Wedgwood, who began to build his reputation for distinctive quality ware from about 1760.

Wedgwood was a dedicated experimentalist, inspired to a great degree by classical design. His most famous innovation was jasperware, an unglazed stoneware stained with strong colours, usually blue or green or black, and embellished in relief with white cameo-like designs. Stoneware also formed the basis of Wedgwood's black

basalt ware and his revival of terracottaware.

Today the most popular examples of pottery to be collected include Staffordshire dogs, toby jugs, and fairings, attractive little ornaments initially given away as prizes at fairs.

PORCELAIN – A BRIEF HISTORY

True porcelain originated in China and seems to have been discovered during the Tang dynasty, AD 618 to 906. It is a very hard ceramic, distinguished from pottery by its translucency.

The Chinese jealously guarded the secret of true porcelain for about 1,000 years and it was not until the 18th century that European manufacture began. Experiments had been carried out for many years until they were succesful in 1710, when deposits of the vital ingredient, kaolin, were discovered in Saxony. The first European porcelain factory was opened at Meissen, near Dresden. The Germans made every effort to prevent rivals in other countries acquiring kaolin and banned its export. Since an attractive imitation porcelain made with glassy substances instead of kaolin had been made since the seventeenth century, European porcelain now developed into two distinct types – hard paste, or true, porcelain, and soft paste.

The majority of English manufacturers continued to work in soft paste until the early 1800s, when Josiah Spode developed bone china.

The manufacture of porcelain in England began between 1743 and 1745 at the London factories of Chelsea and Bow. As the years passed, porcelain-making began in other areas and some great names became established. Among those names is Worcester, which began production in 1751, and Derby, which started up at around the same time. The firm of Coalport, founded in 1796, did not begin to find great fame until around 1820.

The most outstanding and important development in fine English ceramics took place between 1795 and 1820, when soft paste was replaced by a new, superior body, bone china, which was perfected by Josiah Spode of Stoke-on-Trent. It was more durable, had a better finish, and was more stable during manufacture, and by 1820 all the major firms were using it. The Spode factory, founded in 1770, remained a family firm until 1833, when it was purchased by W.T. Copeland.

Another prolific manufacturer of fine china in the nineteenth century was Minton, which made good quality wares at prices within the reach of most people. Minton introduced a dating system in 1824 which makes it of particular interest to collectors, as it allows pieces to be dated to a particular year. The name Rockingham is also synonymous with nineteenth-century china. From about 1820 to the closure of the firm in 1842 Rockingham ware was rarely surpassed in quality. Much of the firm's early output was unmarked and inferior. Other unmarked ware of the period is often wrongly attributed to Rockingham.

DATING POTTERY AND PORCELAIN

Most collectors prefer ceramics which bear some manufacturer's marks, as these clues can often lead to accurate identification and dating. Of course, many items of pottery and porcelain are unmarked and attributing them to a particular manufacturer, or dating them, can be difficult, sometimes impossible, and will certainly require some research.

Unmarked wares can often be dated, but it does require a great deal of expert knowledge about the styles, patterns, and decorative techniques of many different companies. However, when an item does bear a manufacturer's mark, the process can be comparatively easy.

Ceramics are marked in four ways. The first is an *incised* mark made on the clay when it is still soft during manufacture. Under a magnifying glass such marks will have a 'ploughed up' effect. The second method is *impressed* by metal or clay stamps. These give a neat, rather mechanical appearance and the mark used on Wedgwood is probably the best example. *Painted* marks are added over the glaze at the time of decoration. *Printed* marks were transferred from engraved copper plates at the time of decoration. Most nineteenth-century marks are printed.

For the novice, dating pottery and porcelain can sometimes be an extremely frustrating experience. Yet many of the plates, vases and orna-ments scattered around the homes of Britain can be quite easy to date without having any specialist knowledge. This is because most of the items we have at our home, inherited from Auntie Ada or brought on a whim from an antiques shop or antiques fair, are mainly Victorian or early twentieth century. The following information may be helpful in dating such items.

If the word 'Trademark' appears, it denotes a date after 1862, when trademarks were first introduced. Inclusion of the word 'Royal' in a firm's title or trade name indicates a date after 1850, while the use of the word 'Limited' or 'Ltd' means the items must have been made after 1861. Terms which describe the item's pattern are later than 1810 and mostly much later. A common word on plates, vases and other items is 'England', which means the item must have been made after 1891 and probably before about 1920. The term 'Made in England' indicates without doubt twentieth-century manufacture, as does the term 'Bone China' or 'English Bone China'.

While those guidelines can pin an item to a particular period, some items can not only be accurately dated to a single year, but to the actual day of the month. This is because of a system introduced in 1842, when a diamond-shaped registration mark was used on a wide range of ceramics, the shape or pattern of which was registered at the Patent Office. Using a table printed in many ceramic books, you can get a day, month and year date for an item.

In 1884 that system was discontinued and a new one introduced using registered numbers. This method allows dating just to a particular year and was in use until around 1909.

Much of the nineteenth-century pottery and porcelain was made in the Staffordshire Potteries which comprises seven towns – Burslem, Cobridge, Fenton, Hanley, Longton, Stoke, and Tunstall. Many makers in the Potteries used only their initial letters, such as J and G, L, which refers to Jackson and Gosling of Longton. Dating using these initials can be achieved by discovering the manufacturing period of the firms involved. Extensive list of these initials, together with tables relating to registered number dating, can be found in the definitive book on the subject, Geoffrey Godden's *Handbook of Pottery and Porcelain Marks* (Barrie and Jenkins).

Part II

THE COLLECTOR'S A–Z

I was once trading at an antiques fair when a man came up to me and asked if I had any watch keys for sale. Now a watch key, as you may know, is a tiny object about half an inch long and usually available only with the watch it was meant to wind. I replied that I didn't have any watch keys and as that seemed a shade abrupt, I enquired, merely to extend the conversation a little, whether he had a large collection of pocket watches. Matter-of-fact and without a smile, he said, 'I don't own a single watch – I just collect the keys.' And with that he turned and was lost in the crowd.

That incident has stayed vividly in my memory ever since. It serves to remind me that there are no parameters to collecting. People will collect *anything*. What's junk to one is treasure to another. For this reason this A to Z of collecting is far from comprehensive but it does, I believe, cover the primary collecting areas and imparts information on what I believe are the most popular items which seem to attract collectors. Missing, of course, from this listing are watch keys.

ADVERTISING MATERIAL

Advertising material can become dated in a comparatively short time. As a result, advertisements, often linked to the passing fads of a fickle public, mirror intriguing aspects of social behaviour and development. In some ways old advertisements can give a clearer insight into the daily life of the British family than any number of history books and social documents and it is perhaps not surprising that advertising material in its many forms is highly collected.

In addition to the obvious forms of advertising such as posters and enamel street signs, there is greater interest in the art's more subtle manifestations, such as packaging. Cigarette packets, tea caddies and confectionery boxes are now gleefully collected by enthusiasts.

Much advertising material was made of paper or card and was not particularly durable. Surviving examples are therefore at a premium, though this type of material is still less valuable than more solid and lasting types, such as those made of wood, metal or pottery.

Mass marketing techniques and the necessary back-up advertising developed rapidly in the Victorian period and advertising mementos from this era are of great interest. Twentieth-century material also attracts a strong following and advertising techniques change so rapidly that even a 1960s poster can now appear positively archaic.

Some collectors prefer to gather items associated with one particular product such as Hovis, Ovaltine, Oxo, Pear's Soap or perhaps Robertson's jam and marmalade. (Robertsons introduced their range of 'Golly' enamel brooches in 1928).

Many advertising items can still be picked up fairly cheaply, though rare examples are often highly priced. In particular, novelty items are eagerly snapped up. One example which emphasizes how quickly period items can become a collector's piece is the pottery lamp issued by the Guinness Company and featuring their famous toucan. Made not for general sale but to be used as an advertisement on bar counters, these lamps can now fetch £50 or more among enthusiasts.

All items illustrated are inexpensive. The collector of advertising material should not ignore more recent examples.

CECIL ALDIN PRINTS

Dogs are Britain's most popular pets, so it will come as no surprise to learn that prints of our canine chums are also in demand by collectors of old prints. Frequently dog lovers not only like dogs, but models of dogs, books on dogs, and pictures of dogs. And of all the artists who specialized in drawing or painting dogs, none is more sought after and admired than Cecil Aldin.

Aldin was born in Slough, Berkshire, in 1870 and by the age of six was already sketching animals. As he grew older he went to art school and studied animal anatomy. Then he started submitting drawings to magazines and was elated when one was published and he received ten shillings for it.

Ironically, his first published work was not an animal, but was the interior of an inn. But he loved drawing animals, especially dogs, and soon his work was being used in many magazines and newspapers. His reputation grew, both in Britain and America and in the early years of this century he was a household name. He gradually widened the scope of his work and became equally famous for his paintings of sporting scenes and old buildings. But dogs remained his first love and his own pets, Cracker and Micky, were often the subject of his work.

The reason that Aldin's work has proved so durable and so admired even by today's leading artists is that he was able to capture a dog's character and individualism as well. How he did this really lies in his endless study of dogs – the way they stood, sat down, how they slept, yawned, grinned or looked mournful. His own dogs shared his studio and slept on couches, so he was never short of inspiration, and sketched them as they dozed, often in comical positions. The realism and humour of his dog sketches and paintings are remarkable. They ensure that Aldin has a lasting place in the ranks of the most important British artists.

Originals of his work obviously fetch large sums, but there are many of his prints around as they were widely published in the 1920s and 30s, and even since. Aldin himself died in 1935, wealthy, famous, and living in quiet retirement with his beloved dogs.

There have been few more sensitive, or highly collected, portrayers of dogs than Cecil Aldin.

ART DECO

Art Deco was a design movement which took hold immediately after World War I and reached its crescendo in the late 1920s and early 30s. It was a form of rebellion against all design that had gone before and consequently is often more bizarre than it is beautiful. It is a strange mixture of abstract painting, Egyptian and Aztec-style motifs, geometric shapes and patterns, striking colour combinations, and the soft, natural forms of flowers and trees and animals. Like its predecessor, Art Nouveau, it manifests itself in both small, ornamental items and in furniture.

Among the best-known exponents of Art Deco are René Lalique, a Frenchman whose glasswork is particularly admired, and the potter Clarice Cliff, whose off-beat designs and strong use of colour have won her a great following. Work by Lalique can run to thousands of pounds and items by Clarice Cliff (dealt with separately in this book) and a few other top designers will normally run to several hundred pounds.

There is a notable difference between the Art Deco of the 1920s and that of the 1930s. The style of 1920s Art Deco reflects a reaction against the rigours of World War I, manifesting itself in delicate, curvilinear lines. The mood of the 1930s, born out of great world economic problems, was less frivolous and Art Deco of that period has bolder, straighter, more precise lines. Some experts call this latter period, up until 1940, 'Modernist'.

Art Deco items were made however, on a very large scale by other companies and fairly undistinguished pieces of Art Deco can still be found at antiques fairs and in shops for just a few pounds. It is something of an acquired taste, but while many people find it quite ugly, there is no denying that some examples have great beauty.

Examples of less expensive, 1930s Art Deco pottery.

ART NOUVEAU

In the dying years of the Victorian period there was widespread disillusionment with the fussy, often ugly designs that had dominated for several decades. British designers, seeking a new outlet for their artistic talents, turned to nature as a source of inspiration and began to create work with more flowing, simplistic lines. This change of direction was labelled 'Art Nouveau' and seems to have been sparked off by an exhibition of Japanese art held in London in 1862.

It was twenty years or so before these inspirational seeds took strong root, but when they did, it made tremendous impact. Characterized by graceful, almost erotic lines based on plant forms, Art Nouveau swept Europe, and France and Britain in particular took to it with great enthusiasm. In France the most notable exponent was Emile Gallé and in Britain, Rennie Mackintosh, though there were many other designers who also achieved renown.

After 1900 the movement became characterized by what is called its rectilinear phase. Mackintosh was its most brilliant exponent and his work later influenced the Austrians who produced a Viennese version of Art Nouveau. In Britain the new rectilinear style became associated both with the Arts and Crafts Movement and with a revival of the Celtic art of the Dark Ages.

The term Art Nouveau was taken from a shop of that name opened in Paris in 1895 by Samuel Bing. In Germany the style was called *Judgendstil* ('youth style'), in Spain, *Modernista* and in Italy, *Stile Liberty* after the London shop which promoted the new designs.

These days, examples of Art Nouveau are highly sought after and prices tend to be high, because the movement was short-lived, killed off by the First World War.

Art Nouveau manifests itself not only in small objects such as vases and clocks, but in furniture, too. Prices can vary enormously. Some work by Gallé, for instance, can command sums between £5,000 and £10,000. Most Art Nouveau furniture will certainly fetch several hundred pounds, and often a great deal more, depending on the novelty and beauty of the design. But there are still small examples of Art Nouveau much lower down the price scale, largely because they were originally mass-produced. Even so, they are still collected. But there are still many fairly attractive, but routine items available for well under £50.

Examples of the graceful, flowing lines of Art Nouveau craftsmanship.

AUTOMATA

Automata is the term applied to what are in effect adult toys; mechanical figures, human or animal, which have a rather robot-like quality. Surprisingly the history of these intricate devices dates back several centuries, with a primitive example apparently existing as early as 1250.

It was, however, from about 1600 onwards that mechanical musical models began to appear more widely, usually in the homes of the very wealthy. Some appeared so life-like, that the makers were accused of sorcery. The figures were made to move by similar mechanical means to those which power clocks and, to give additional interest to mere movement, a musical function was usually provided. Because of the close association with clock making, many types of automata contained a time piece and this was particularly so during the nineteenth century when examples became much more elaborate. Many of these were mounted under large domes and incorporated scenes such as ships sailing across the ocean, soldiers riding horses over a bridge, windmills and water wheels turning and even miniature orchestras playing.

Another popular form of automata was the singing bird, usually in a gilded cage. The first examples were made in Switzerland as early as 1752 and they reached a peak of popularity in the middle of the last century. The birds were made to sing by means of small bellows which were opened and closed by clockwork and thus pumped air to a whistle which had its notes varied by means of a piston. Additional mechanical features allowed the birds not only to move their heads and flap their wings but in some cases actually flutter from branch to branch. While nineteenth-century examples are obviously expensive, the singing bird has continued to be manufactured since and I have known a number of people taken in by quite modern examples which have been falsely aged.

As the nineteenth century drew to a close, musical automata became less intricate and took on more of a novelty value. Small musical movements were fitted into dolls, toy animals, jewellery boxes, cigarette boxes and photograph albums. Modern examples continue to be made, with the musical toilet roll holder perhaps the worst example to come to mind, epitomizing to many the height of poor taste.

An example of Victorian automata. The lid rises and a whistling bird emerges.

BRUCE BAIRNSFATHER

The man whom many feel did most to help win World War I was not a great general, not even a VC hero. He was a cartoonist.

Bruce Bairnsfather boosted the morale of troops in the trenches with his witty, sharply observed and highly amusing cartoons. Throughout the grim conflict Bairnsfather's stream of drawings put smiles on the faces of the soldiers. Now his work is recognized as classic and his cartoons are sought by collectors.

Bairnsfather, born in 1888, went into the Army after leaving school but quit to try to make a living as an artist. His talents were used for drawing advertisements, without much success, until he rejoined the Army in 1914 when the Great War started. Amazed by the good humour of troops risking death under heavy fire, he began to draw cartoons to amuse his fellow soldiers and eventually sent an example of his work to a magazine. They liked it, paid him the then large fee of three guineas, and asked for more.

Soon after, Bairnsfather was injured by a shell explosion and had more time to draw cartoons during his convalescence. They appeared as a series called *Fragments from France*, were instant bestsellers and made Bairnsfather famous. One of the characters he created, an archetypal soldier known as Old Bill, was the subject of many cartoons and was even revived during World War II.

Though Bairnsfather is best remembered as a humorist, his artistic talent ran much deeper and he was the official war artist for the American Government during the last war. He died in 1959 aged 71. Books of his work from the Great War still turn up in antique shops and can be picked up for just a few pounds. While his cartoons are popular with collectors, there is much more demand for Bairnsfather mementos made in pottery or china. His fame is such that many pottery firms turned out plates, mugs, vases and models featuring some of his best known cartoons. Though they were made cheaply and were sold for very little when new, prices are steadily soaring as more and more collectors appreciate their significance.

Although many pottery firms used Bairnfather's designs for their work, their collecting value is still steadily increasing.

BANKNOTES

'I have a £1 note here,' said the man, 'will anyone give me £300 for it?' Someone raised a hand and as the bidding went to £400, hands kept waving. Finally, at £500 the auctioneer's hammer crashed down. 'Sold,' he said with finality.

Anyone willing to pay £500 for a £1 note is either a lunatic or very knowledgeable, and in the case I've mentioned at a banknote sale in London, the buyer was a collector who knew exactly what he was doing. He was investing money in money. Old banknotes are one way of proving that it is not always a case of the shrinking pound. Banknote collectors are prepared to pay a small fortune for rare examples.

Banknotes have a rather colourful history. Until about 1850 any bank could issue notes payable to the bearer on demand. Consequently, many banknotes were 'local', issued by a bank in a particular town or district. Since there were scores of private banks scattered around the country, the scope for banknote collecting is great.

Because these old notes are no longer legal tender, their collectors' value is not really related to their face value. While a £1 note can be worth £500, a £50 note might be worth only £1. What determines value is rarity. Keen collectors, who incidentally are often bank managers or financiers, will pay high sums for little known banknotes. Most of these date back to the seventeenth and eighteenth century.

After 1850 only the Bank of England and a few Scottish banks could issue their own notes. Real rarities occur when notes are issued for special reasons, or were withdrawn after a short time. Once such case was when the Treasury issued a £1 note to be used in the Dardanelles campaign during World War I. The campaign failed and the notes were withdrawn within a few days. Banknotes relating to that event can now top £500 each.

'Fractional' banknotes, having a face value of just a few shillings, were issued during World War I and II in case there was a shortage of coins. These notes, too, can command high prices.

Collecting old money doesn't require you to be rich in order to indulge. Some banknotes can be fairly cheap. Provincial banknotes such as those issued by the Norfolk and Suffolk General Bank in the early 1800s still fetch under £50 and other notes cost even less. Banknotes which have long been withdrawn, but were common in their day, still have a collectors' value, though not a great deal. The large £1, £5 and £10 notes issued before and after the last war are now worth up to £50 each these days, though condition and rarity can increase or reduce these figures. Even the ten shilling note which was withdrawn from circulation in 1962 has now increased in value to the extent that collectors will pay several pounds for an example in mint condition.

Rarity, not face value is the key to banknote collecting.

BAROMETERS

The weather has no doubt always been a talking point and so it is hardly surprising that any instrument which could help predict the weather would prove welcome. Primitive forms of barometer existed as scientific instruments many centuries ago but it was not until about 1690 that they came into domestic use.

Essentially, there are two kinds of barometer – the stick and the wheel. The stick type, two or three feet long and just two or three inches wide, is the most revered by collectors, being the earliest, best made and most accurate type. Both used the rise and fall of mercury in a glass tube to indicate weather changes. The stick type utilized a long straight tube placed against a graduated scale, while the wheel variety used a tube in the shape of an inverted siphon. The mercury was linked to a needle which could swing around a circular dial.

Barometer design is closely allied to that of longcase clocks and the same woods are used: walnut, ebony, rosewood and oak. Eighteenth-century barometers tended to be on the plain side while nineteenth-century examples became decorative, with carving and inlay.

Barometers were expensive items and only the wealthy could afford them, but from about 1850 barometers became cheaper, more widespread, largely due to the introduction of the aneroid type which operated not by mercury but from air pressure on a vacuum chamber. This is the method still used for modern barometers.

Good eighteenth- and early nineteenth-century mercury barometers are expensive but Victorian and Edwardian aneroid examples are much more common and not that costly. It is worth bearing in mind that if you come across a mercury barometer requiring repair it can be a very expensive process. Frequently the glass tube and mercury have to be replaced and this is highly specialized work.

A typical Victorian banjo barometer with a classical pediment and a mercury room thermometer.

BOARD GAMES

Board games date back thousands of years with the first 'boards' being a piece of flat rock or parched earth. Most games appear to have religious origins, some stemming from practices of divination. It was in the eighteenth and nineteenth centuries that board games became popular in Britain and became more associated with children than adults. Many of these games were produced to supplement a child's education and featured aspects of geography, nature and scripture.

By Victorian times games were increasingly being produced only for amusement. A large number of games had short-lived popularity and are now long forgotten and of interest only to collectors in this field. Other games have had a timeless appeal and two best examples of this are Snakes and Ladders which originated in India and was introduced into Britain in the middle of the last century, and Ludo, also from India, and apparently making its debut here in 1896.

Much of the fun in collecting these old games is in seeing how they reflect changing times and important events. Famous battles, pastimes such as horse racing, big game hunting and even events such as the great Klondyke Gold Rush of the 1890s were used as suitable subjects for board games.

Victorian and Edwardian games of this kind have so far not attracted the same level of attention as dolls and clockwork toys of the same period and thus prices are not at 'heady' levels and there is plenty of scope for the novice collector. By and large this is also true of other games and pastimes such as jigsaw puzzles (introduced in their present form in about 1840), various card games and favourites such as Mah Jong. However, interest – and prices – rise when it comes to games such as Backgammon, Cribbage and ones using dice and gaming counters. The reason for this is that such games usually came in a more durable form utilizing decorative wooden boxes and boards, which have additional appeal to collectors.

Recently renewed popular interest in new games will almost certainly lead to an increase in the value of earlier boardgames.

BOOKS

Many people have old books in their possession and tend to believe that because they are dated a century or more ago, they must be quite valuable. Alas, this is rarely the case. Many factors determine which books are collected and therefore valuable. Age can often be the least important.

What is of concern to a collector is the subject of the book, the author, perhaps the illustrator, and even the type of binding. First editions are sought after, of course, but every book published has a first edition. Only the books that achieved some degree of success in their time are really in demand.

Books have always been published in fairly large numbers and even those published some 200 years ago are still sufficiently common to be worth very little. Boxes of Victorian books can still be purchased in local auctions for as little as £1 for several dozen.

Certain subjects have special interest to collectors and these include scientific matters, natural history, travel and exploration. There is more chance of a non-fiction book being of interest to a collector than a novel, as many novelists are no longer remembered. Some Victorian fiction is collected, but not because of its literary merit. Victorian novels frequently had beautifully illustrated covers and is the reason they are sought.

There is something of a collector's market too for books of a much more recent vintage – early hardbacks by P.G. Wodehouse, for instance, and even first editions of the Biggles stories by Captain W.E. Johns.

One book which people feel is always valuable is an old Bible. Family Bibles have often been handed down from generation to generation and are mostly in excellent condition even when 200 or more years old. Yet the Bible has always been a best seller, so millions of them were printed, even two centuries ago. Bibles have also been looked after with more care than most books, and so have survived in great numbers. Consequently, they are worth rather less than you might expect. There is a market for leather-bound, brass-clasped family bibles, but they are not yet fetching great sums.

Collectors though can still live in hope. The Gospels of Henry the Lion, an 800 year-old illustrated book, was sold by Sotheby's in 1983 for a staggering £9,000,000, made up of a bid of £7,400,000 and a buyer's premium of an additional £600,000. The book was brought on behalf of the West German government. The book originated in Germany in the twelfth century.

Illustrated books are frequently more valuable than non-illustrated examples or even first editions, particularly if the artist is well-known.

BOTTLES

While bottle collecting has been with us for some years, enthusiasm has now peaked and begun to decline. This means, however, that those who still collect are true enthusiasts and it is their purchasing power that makes some old bottles very valuable.

Bottles make a fascinating collection, colourful, interesting, and a mirror of the changing social habits in Britain. The hobby falls into two distinct sections, the very expensive and the very cheap.

Rare bottles tend to date back to the 1600s and are often wine containers complete with the private seal of the owner embossed in the glass. Between 1623 and 1860 it was illegal to sell wine by the bottle in Britain and there was a high tax on the use of glass. Wine was therefore bought by the barrel and decanted into private bottles bearing the name, initials or crest of the owner, and sometimes a date. Such bottles are regularly unearthed as the sites of nineteenth-century rubbish dumps are uncovered by building development.

The most common bottle of the Victorian age was the marble-in-the-neck variety, the marble being used as a seal to keep the mineral water fizzy. These have great novelty value, but are not worth very much. Examples can still be picked up for £2 or £3, though some rarer examples in different colours or with special designs can be worth rather more.

Another method used to keep the 'fizz' and freshness in bottles was the crown cork bottle which utilized a cork-lined metal cap; screw stoppers as well as lever stoppers are not uncommon.

Chinese snuff bottles represent a specialized area of bottle collection that can occasionally bring items of great beauty and value to the enthusiast. These little bottles which come in a variety of shapes have a cork or stopper to which a tiny spoon is connected, which projects into the bottle. The spoons are usually made of bone, ivory or wood. The bottles themselves are fashioned from a number of materials – porcelain, jade, glass, amber, rock crystal and carved red lacquer. They vary in price from a few pounds to several hundred, and, on occasions, thousands of pounds.

Among the many different types of bottles collected, those used for storing poisons are of special interest, as are those meant to contain perfume.

Bottles present a wide and inexpensive field for the collector. Note the blue poison bottle in the forefront and the Victorian 'pop' bottle on its right.

BRASS AND COPPER

The mellow glow from highly polished brass or copper items is one of the most attractive sights in antique furnishings. Many homes in Britain have at least one, and often dozens, of items made from these humble metals. Yet the one question about brass and copper that baffles almost everyone is: how can you tell the age?

Metals, I need hardly point out, show little sign of wear and most objects made from brass and copper have no makers' names or numbers. The only way to estimate age is by the construction or design.

Until the seventeenth century brass and copper was mostly imported into Britain, often from the Far East. But during the 1700s it became an increasingly important manufacturing industry in this country. Early pieces were of fairly simple construction, mostly solid castings, but as techniques improved, methods of rolling brass and copper into thin sheets were devised. Rolled brass came into widespread use from about 1730, while methods of spinning brass into shapes took another fifty years to perfect. Machine stamping – mostly used for such items as furniture handles – dates from about 1770.

Much brass and copperware was made for use in the kitchen. Saucepans, kettles, jugs, measures, jelly moulds and jam pans are just a few of the household items in widespread use during the last century. The fireplace was a prime position for brass and copper. Fenders, pokers, shovels and coal scuttles were made and other domestic wares included oil lamps, candlesticks, door knockers, finger plates, curtain rods, stair rods, door handles and simple ornaments.

Late in the Victorian period, brass and copper began to be ousted from the kitchen by enamelware, and by early this century the great boom for brass and copper was over. The industry has survived in much smaller form and there is a great market today for reproduction items such as oil lamps, kettles, wall plaques and coal bins, to name but a few.

Brass and copper can easily be given a rather aged appearance by use of certain chemicals, so it is worth questioning the vendor about authenticity when purchasing.

The Victorians with their unabashed love of decoration were fond collectors of brass and copperware, and in particular ornamented screens, including firescreens.

BRONZE

To the trained eye bronze is a very distinct material, but to those who are not expert, it can sometimes be confused with heavily tarnished brass or even spelter, a light alloy widely used in the latter half of the last century.

Bronze is an alloy made from copper and tin and is dark brown in colour. It has a history going back thousands of years, but it was not until the eighteenth and nineteenth centuries that it became widely popular as a means of making decorative items. The nineteenth century in particular saw large-scale production of bronzes, mostly in the form of classical figures and groups featuring birds and animals. The French in particular specialized in animal bronzes and these became immensely popular from about 1830 to the turn of the century. Britain, Russia, Germany and Italy also turned out bronze sculpture on a smaller scale. Many sculptures, particularly larger ones, are often signed or initialled by the sculptor and, like paintings, such work is valued on the merits of the artist.

Smaller examples of bronze, particularly figures, are especially collected, though there is some confusion in this field. What many people believe is bronze turns out to be either spelter or some other metal with a painted bronze finish, and worth comparatively little. Genuine bronze is a heavy material, but unfortunately so is brass, and discoloured, heavily tarnished brass is sometimes mistaken for bronze.

Another confusing factor is that modern technology has allowed a bronze-like resin to be made which, when weighted inside with lead, can appear to be genuine bronze. This resin is mostly used to reproduce small signed animals and figures and can sometimes be so good that experts can be fooled. The usual giveaway for these fakes is the price. Even small signed bronze sculptures that are genuine are likely to cost a few hundred pounds. The fakes are frequently on offer at little more than £50.

A nineteenth-century French bronze.

BUTTON HOOKS

Button hooks are among the most popular items collected by women, but few know that these dainty devices, a symbol of femininity, were originally made for use by men. It was not delicate ladies' buttoned boots which sparked off the button hook boom, but a fashion among men in the early nineteenth century for stiff, leather boots with a multi-button fastening. The buttons were far too small and numerous to fasten by hand, so the button hook was invented to avoid fumbling.

Like any fashion accessory, the button hook, humble instrument though it was, could be a miniature work of art in itself. While early examples were plain with simple wooden handles, others were made for the wealthy and had silver or ivory handles with engraving and decoration.

Around 1850 women took to wearing high, buttoned boots. Bending over to fasten them was a problem for these ladies due to their boned corsets, so they too took to using button hooks, and theirs were much more decorative than mens'. Some were in the form of characters such as Mr Punch, William Shakespeare or even Dick Turpin. Others were modelled on animals, birds or even reptiles. Some commemorated special events such as coronations or exhibitions, along with major cities, resorts and sporting themes.

They were also used in publicity for advertising products such as polish, tea, coffee, cakes, condensed milk, footwear or clothing. Button hooks were not confined to use on boots and shoes. Smaller button hooks were used for fastening elbow-length buttoned gloves which were fashionable until the early years of this century.

Many people are surprised that the button hook flourished into the twentieth century, but the reason is simple enough. The Edwardian period saw a boom in the popularity of leisure activities such as cycling, horse riding and motoring, leading to an increased demand for sensible, buttoned boots. After the First World War fashions began to change, and while the button hook lingered until the 1930s, it finally died. In 1947 and 1948 buttoned shoes came briefly back into fashion and shops gave away plastic-handled button hooks, but it was a short-lived revival.

Period button hooks are still fairly common, with plain examples costing just a pound or two, but rarer designs can command higher sums, depending on the keenness of collectors to acquire them. Some collectors, of course, are completely hooked.

Ivory and silver-handled button hooks. The smaller hooks of more delicate construction were often used to secure glove buttons.

CAMERAS

Demand for cameras from the early years of photography has risen rapidly in recent years and has pushed up the price of some vintage equipment to more than a thousand pounds.

The first photographic image was produced in 1816, but it was many years later that the camera in the form we know it today came into use. In 1839 a Frenchman called Daguerre marketed a simple box camera which could produce pictures on specially treated glass plates. Although Daguerrotypes, as they were known, remained popular throughout the 1850s, they were overtaken by technical developments, notably the introduction of the wet plate camera, which reigned supreme until 1879 when Kodak introduced dry plate equipment. This simplified the whole photographic process and led to a large number of firms manufacturing their own equipment.

In 1896 cameras were produced with a bellows fitment and this led to much more accurate shutter speeds. This type of camera remained very popular between the wars and even these are now becoming collected.

Early cameras are highly sought after and command very high prices, but some cameras don't have to be all that old to be valuable. Rare models, particularly the post-war Zeiss and Leica models, are now beginning to fetch high prices. One of the rarest Leica models is their 250 reporter's camera, a pocket-sized camera which cost a few pounds when new, but which now commands a staggering £2,000 to £3,000.

Domestic cameras of the 1920s and 30s have picked up in price in the last five years, some now fetching around £25 each, and even the utterly simple Kodak Brownie models of the 1950s are beginning to turn up at antiques fairs and in shops at around a fiver. Just a couple of years ago, dealers were throwing them away. Obviously someone has put them in the picture.

Early twentieth-century cameras including a large studio camera. Note the late Victorian gilt and velvet frame, also collected.

CARRIAGE CLOCKS

We take the wristwatch for granted today, but in the early nineteenth century the wealthy had to carry a clock around with them. It was a rather special clock, designed to be small, easy to transport and reliable enough to withstand the rough roads of Regency England. Not surprisingly it was called the carriage clock.

These delicate clocks, usually brass cased, glass panelled and with a small carrying handle, have become classic time-pieces. Early examples can fetch thousands of pounds. Indeed, at least one has topped £50,000. But because these clocks were so popular, they were made long after the need for them had faded. Victorian examples, produced by a semi-mass production method, attracted large sales and though they look as good as earlier models, production quality is somewhat poor.

Even in Edwardian times the carriage clock was still popular and though demand has declined this century, modern examples are still manufactured, looking much the same as they did more than a century ago.

The man who originated carriage clocks was probably a Frenchman called Abraham Louis Breguet. He appears to have made the first example which he called *pendule de voyage* about 1810. It was a rather complicated device which included a calendar and a temperature device. His concept of a small, mobile clock however, became popular. Being designed for transport, they were often in their own wooden or leather travelling cases to protect them from the rigours of the journey. When not in transit, the clock would adorn a mantelpiece or other item of furniture and it is this multi-role which has resulted in a popularity spanning almost two centuries.

The best example were almost always French, being rather more delicate in appearance and therefore prettier. English clocks have a heavy-looking appearance, though the movements were highly accurate. Because the clocks were so small – average height only 13-15 cm (5–6 in), and I have seen some only 5 cm (2 in) tall – the faces had to be simply and clearly marked in order to be seen across a dimly lit room. Roman numerals were invariably used on plain white backgrounds, with the hands being sharply defined even if decorated.

Because the general design of carriage clocks has remained virtually unaltered over the years, dating can be a problem. Often the only clues are small design features which sometimes varied in line with current fashions.

Highly decorative cases always command higher prices, but the main factor in assessing price is the quality and complexity of the movement. Obviously non-chiming examples are less sought after and the more complicated a chime system, the more a collector will pay.

A nineteenth-century carriage clock with a typical sparsely-ornamented, rectangular gilt case and simple face.

CHILDREN'S BOOKS

The potential collector of children's books will not have to delve too far into the past to build and enhance his collection for many valuable works of this kind are comparatively recent publications.

There has been a tremendous boom in collecting children's books in the last few years and prices are rising fast. And interest is not just confined to first editions. The illustrators of certain books can provide the basis of their value. Artists such as Louis Wain, Arthur Rackham and Kate Greenway are themselves highly collected and if they provided the illustrations for particular children's books, it adds greatly to the demand for those books.

While many people must feel that only first editions of classics such as *Alice in Wonderland* or *Winnie the Pooh* fetch large sums, this is not the case. At a London saleroom quite recently a first edition of Richard Adams' *Watership Down*, published in 1972, fetched several hundred pounds.

There are many other examples of relatively recent books fetching heady prices. The books of Beatrix Potter, for instance, have always been a special delight to collectors and first editions can be quite valuable. A 1902 copy of *The Tailor of Gloucester* will fetch £600 to £800, and a copy of her classic *The Fairy Caravan*, published in 1919, as much as £1,000. This is astonishing when you consider that a really early children's book such as Thomas Beswick's 1771 publication, *A New Lottery of Birds and Beasts*, a book to help children learn the alphabet, will fetch only £300 to £400.

In many cases, the older a book is, the less interest it excites, as the authors have often faded from public memory. Yet children's stories like *The Wind In The Willows*, *Winnie The Pooh*, *Alice in Wonderland* and many more, will probably stay popular for ever, and collectors will always want early copies.

Children's annuals, which first became popular in Victorian times, are also eagerly sought after these days, though collectors favour the pre-war annuals such a *Film Fun, Tiger Tim* and others. Even early editions of annuals like *The Dandy* and *The Beano* are beginning to creep up in price. Who collects them? Many are middle-aged people, who want reminders of their youth. Collecting children's books is certainly not kids' stuff.

'Prize' books, tales of deering-do and kindergarten picture books are still available cheaply.

CHINESE PORCELAIN

It is fair to say that even with advances in science and technology, today's potter only occasionally achieves the perfection of the Chinese potter of earlier times. And of all the achievements of the Chinese potter, porcelain must rank as the greatest.

Porcelain was first discovered in China during the later years of the T'ang dynasty (AD 618–906). It was made by fusing a mixture of china clay (kaolin) and china stone (petuntse). What makes porcelain so different from other ceramics is the fact that both the body and the glaze (also made from petuntse) contain a material called feldspar, and that when the two are fired together they fuse leaving no distinction between the body and the glaze.

Much Chinese porcelain is a hard, white, translucent ceramic, but they also made a hard, dusky and grey material which had been fired to such a vitrifiable state that it emitted a musical note when struck. Celadon ware is the best example of this, having a beautiful translucent green glaze, imitative of jade, with a velvety texture.

The Chinese potter used two methods of painted decoration – underglaze and overglaze. 'Blue and white' porcelain is perhaps the most popularly known example of underglaze painting, and it is this style that so many countries later tried to copy. They were invariably only partly successful because the Chinese ores and minerals used for this effect contained impurities which could not be reproduced elsewhere. This, combined with the particular skills of the Chinese potter produced a unique effect.

Blue and white porcelain from the K'ang Hsi dynasty (1662-1722) is considered to be the best; later wares were progressively inferior, though given the unsurpassed nature of the best porcelains are still highly collectable.

The Chinese porcelain trade with Europe began as early as the mid-sixteenth century. The Dutch later traded extensively in Ming blue and white; the emperor K'ang Hsi extended this trade to other countries.

Reign marks are rarely found on K'ang Hsi wares, only on nineteenth century or later wares. Most of the porcelain found in this country are eighteenth- or nineteenth-century examples. Later nineteenth-century examples can be found for less than £100.

A selection of eighteenth- and nineteenth-century Chinese porcelains.

CIGARETTE CARDS

Large-scale manufacture of cigarettes began in Britain in the 1860s, but it was to be another twenty years before the craze for cigarette cards began. It first caught on in America, where manufacturers had been boosting sales of cigarettes by including in the packet a card depicting a pretty girl, mostly actresses and famous beauties of the day.

The first major British company to utilize cigarette cards seems to have been W.H. and H.O. Wills. Though the first cards what Wills issued merely advertised their own cigarettes, they too turned to illustrations of pretty girls, and then other themes followed.

Once the trend had started, there seemed no stopping it. Almost every conceivable subject was used for cigarette cards, until the outbreak of World War II finally put an end to their production. There were cards showing soldiers, ships, motor cars, arms and crests of the nobility, Victoria Cross heroes, radio and music hall stars, air raid precautions, royalty, flowers, wildlife, military uniforms, famous buildings, historical events, flags of the world – the list was virtually endless.

Today, these sets are highly collected and while most sets are worth just a few pounds, rare and early sets can command hundreds of pounds to the keenest collectors. Sets must be complete and in good condition to interest a collector. Preferably they should also be loose, not stuck to the pages of albums which were often provided by cigarette manufactures. Album sets normally have a lesser value, usually under £5, unless it is a particularly sought-after set.

Complete sets of cigarette cards housed in albums are still inexpensive collectables.

CLARICE CLIFF

Of all the names associated with the Art Deco period of the 1920s and 1930s, that of Clarice Cliff is by far the best known. Her pottery designs are startlingly original, brightly, almost garishly coloured, and surprisingly valuable.

She was born in Tunstall, Stoke-on-Trent, in 1899 and after going to art school in nearby Burslem, was apprenticed to a local pottery company. Never afraid to experiment with colour and unusual shape, her work has a distinctive quality which is easily recognized even among the many rather odd designs which proliferated in the Art Deco period.

Most of Clarice Cliff's output was of a very practical nature, such as tea-sets and vases. Her early work is the most sought after and really centres on just two of her ranges, the Bizarre and Fantasque series. With these ranges, utilizing vivid shades of orange, yellow, blue, red and green, she was at her most uninhibited.

It is common for a vase, Bizarre or Fantasque to fetch well over £1,000 and even a small item like a pencil holder to fetch £200 or £300. While complete tea services are eagerly sought by collectors and also fetch several hundred pounds, even single items from such sets are in demand, though in a much lower price range. Clarice Cliff also designed a series called Biarritz, which featured items of rectangular shape and though made in fewer numbers than the Bizarre and Fantasque ranges, attract similar prices.

Clarice Cliff items carry her transfer-printed signature on the base and this makes identification a relatively easy task. Sadly, she died in 1972 just as collecting interest in her work was gathering pace.

A selection of Clarice Cliff ware, including a piece from her Crocus series (centre) and a vase from her Bizarre range.

CLOCKWORK TOYS

Clockwork toys became established in Europe in the 1880s with the French and Germans leading the way in manufacturing, with Britain close behind. They were usually cheaply made, cheaply sold items. Many of these toys were flimsily constructed and had a very short life in the hands of energetic and destructive children and that fact is the key to the amazingly high value that surviving examples have today.

There have been a number of examples of Edwardian clockwork cars topping £1,000 when sold at auction and some have made more than £2,000 each. Even less scarce and less perfect examples of early clockwork vehicles can fetch several hundred pounds each and demand seems to be growing all the time. Mostly they bear the names of German manufacturers such as Bing, Carette, Marklin, Stutz and Schuco. There are also a number of French manufacturers whose wares attract high prices and they include Decamps, JEP and Martin.

Most early forms of clockwork toys were in the forms of animals or human figures, but once the motor car had been invented and then the aeroplane, manufacturers seemed to concentrate on these.

Of course, condition plays a vital part in the value of clockwork toys which are normally made of tin-plate. Apart from being bendable and breakable, they are also prone to rusting. Thus mint examples, often in their original boxes, can fetch breath-taking prices. Scratched, dented and battered examples are not so eagerly sought as restoration is not only difficult but frequently impossible.

The price levels of early clockwork toys are now such that they are really beyond the scope of the novice collector and this has helped increase demand for toys from a later period, Such toys from the 1930s have become increasingly expensive and this, together with the use of today of plastic for making toys, have helped make even tin-plate clockwork toys from the 1950s, 1960s and even early 1970s of interest to collectors. In particular, clockwork toys made in Japan, even as recently as the 1970s and featuring robots and space-craft, are now attracting collectors, with prices rising steadily. Today's novice collector of clockwork has to be comparatively well-off in order to maintain his hobby, and would-be collectors of limited means are increasingly turning to die-cast models like Dinky toys, which are dealt with in this book under a separate heading.

A collection of clockwork toys covering some sixty years. Few British examples were made before World War I. Even recent Japanese toys such as robots, are now highly collectable.

COINS

Few areas of antiques are more clouded with myth and misunderstanding than coins. Everyone comes across old coins from time to time and hopes are often raised that they may be quite valuable. Well, they might be, but don't count on it.

What people fail to understand is just how important *condition* is when it comes to coin collecting. For example, the rarest Victorian penny is dated 1869, when comparatively few were made. A mint example is worth about £300, yet a well-circulated example is worth little more than 50 pence. This astonishing difference occurs because collectors require coins only in first-class order and are simply not interested in well-worn examples.

Coins are graded according to condition and a 'fine' example is, to a collector, one of the worst grades. In fact 'fine' means there is considerable wear on the upper surfaces. 'Very fine' means slight traces of wear on the raised surfaces, while 'extremely fine' means coins which appear to have been uncirculated but still display slight marks or tiny scratches on the surface. 'Uncirculated' may sound as if it is the top grade, but it is not. Even unissued coins can, due to modern production methods, have faint manufacturing flaws. 'Fleur-de-coin' is the ultimate state of the coin – unused, in mint condition, and without any marks or signs of wear.

Of course, age is the other important factor, and one myth I must demolish is that the older the coin, the more its value. This simply isn't true. A leading London coin expert told me: 'There are plenty of Roman coins which are worthless. The Roman economy was very sophisticated and very much money-orientated. Huge amounts of Roman coins have survived and despite their great age, are worth only pence each.'

Much more recent coins can fetch far more than Roman or medieval examples, provided that they are scarce because of a low mint, and are in top condition. Sotheby's have sold a 1937 British coin for £2,900 – and in better condition it might have made as much as £10,000. The coin in question was a silver florin and the reason for it having such a high value was because it bore the head of King Edward VIII. Edward VIII abdicated just a couple of weeks before the coins were issued and though many thousands had been made, they were recalled and destroyed. But a small number did survive, mostly given as mementos to staff at the Royal Mint. The example sold at Sotheby's belonged to the man who designed it.

One final point that is most important: never clean old coins. You can devalue them dramatically if you do. Even gently immersing them in water can damage some coins and what cleaning can be done must be left to experts.

The vast majority of old coins, both British and Foreign, are worth very little to collectors, but if you do have a quantity of old coins, it is obviously worth having them examined by a coin dealer, just in case you do have a rarity.

Old or new, coins can be both valuable and collectable.

COMICS

Back in the 1950s when I was a small boy, I was, like most kids, comic mad. I read the *Beano*, *Dandy*, *Topper*, *Beezer*, *Victor*, and any others I could lay my hands on. I revelled in the adventures of Desperate Dan, Dennis the Menace, Lord Snooty, and even such strange characters as Little Plum, your redskin chum.

I can recall an old uncle giving me copies of his boyhood comics such as the *Gem*, *Magnet*, *Film Fun*, *Radio Fun*, and various others. I read them all and then cheerfully threw them away. That has turned out to be a big mistake, for if only I had kept them, their value today would pay for a holiday.

Nostalgia for those far-off days of boyhood when there seemed to be blazing sunshine every holiday, when Arthur Askey was the funniest man on earth and a new Ford car was just a hundred pounds, has resulted in a huge army of collectors of old comics which bring back memories of the youth of yesteryear.

Keen collectors will pay as much as £20 for some copies of pre-war comics and more than £50 for rare examples, and I have heard of some changing hands for well over £100.

The comic market divides neatly into two categories: the pre-war British publications and the imported American offerings such as *Superman*, *Captain Marvel*, *Batman*, *Tarzan*, and other characters. The British comics do, I feel, have more charm and certainly more innocence. They were first produced at the turn of the century and some of the characters like Tiger Tim and Teddy Tail retained their popularity for more than a half a century. Indeed, Tiger Tim is still going strong. Other comics, like the *Gem* and the *Magnet*, introduced such characters as Billy Bunter, and in the 1930s and 40s *Film Fun* and *Radio Fun* comics featured the adventures of popular film comedians and radio celebrities. Now, even comics from the 1950s and 60s are becoming collected, especially those that are linked with TV characters.

The American comics were also very popular in Britain and these appeal to a different type of collector who appreciates the comic strip artistry. Superman made his debut in 1938 in *Action* comic and went on to have his own comic. Incidentally, the two men who created Superman sold the rights to him for about £50 before he became really famous. He went on to make millions for the new owners of the copyright.

America also produced a vast range of horror story comics in the 1950s which were successful for about five years, until there was a public outcry about the violence in them. Critics claimed they caused juvenile crime. These comics are now in demand by collectors.

Anyone who has old comics really needs to sell them to a specialist dealer or to put them in auctions held at Christie's or Sotheby's.

Comics such as these, often by noted artists, can still be found for under £1 and are worth holding on to.

CORKSCREWS

It was in the seventeenth century that corks became the most popular method of preserving liquid in a bottle. The invention of the corkscrew was obviously an immediate necessity. Although all corkscrews essentially perform the same function, it is the variation on the method used that fascinates collectors.

Many different kinds of corkscrew were patented, particularly in the nineteenth century. Some were spring loaded, some used clamps, some had safety devices, and others performed further functions such as opening tins. Generally the more intricate and unusual the corkscrew as well as the more ornate, the greater its collecting value.

While the spiral section of corkscrews was invariably made of steel, the handles utilized a wide range of materials. Gold handles were rare, while silver ones were popular in the eighteenth and nineteenth centuries; nickel, bronze and electroplate examples are quite common. In addition, horn, ivory, bone, mother-of-pearl were used, and of course wood, either turned or carved. Early in the twentieth century glass handles, sometimes with *millefiori* decoration in the manner of paperweights, were popular. Porcelain and pottery examples, however, are comparatively rare.

Of particular interest to corkscrew buffs are the novelty models, which have unusual handles. These often take the form of human faces, complete figures, like young nude girls, the heads of animals or even ships. Many different varieties of Victorian and Edwardian corkscrews are still available cheaply but older and more unusual types can fetch a couple of hundred pounds or more.

The charm of corkscrews, as well as their collecting value, lies in their often imaginative handles, such as the silver elephant shown here.

CORONATIONWARE

The first coronation souvenir was issued as early as 1546, a special medal for the coronation of Edward VI. From the middle of the seventeenth century, coronation commemoratives began to be made in glass and ceramics. Obviously, early examples are rare and priceless and are outside the scope of the ordinary collector.

It is not until the nineteenth century that we begin to find coronationware at a price range that may be affordable. Three coronations took place within seventeen years in the nineteenth century: those of George IV, William IV and Queen Victoria. Items relating to any of these three coronations are extremely scarce and unlikely to turn up at the typical antiques fair or local antiques shop.

While souvenirs were made in the form of jugs, plates, bowls, vases and figures, the coronation mug is by far the most popular with collectors. A mug dating from Queen Victoria's coronation in 1837, even with perhaps cracks or minor chips will still fetch several hundred pounds, though happily, mugs from her two jubilees in 1887 and 1897 are rather more plentiful and considerably cheaper.

Many factors come into play when determining the value of mugs or other ceramic souvenirs. Items made in porcelain and by quality manufacturers are worth more than those made in pottery, for instance. The coronation of King Edward VII in 1902 produced a large number of commemorative items. His coronation was postponed from June 26 to August 9 because the king was taken ill with appendicitis. Look out for items bearing the August date. They are much rarer and eagerly collected.

Edward VIII was not actually crowned as king, but the pottery industry had been making souvenirs for months in anticipation of the great event and, as I said earlier, such souvenirs are still available in great numbers, and have no special value just because of the abdication.

There is also an interesting market for the more novel souvenirs, cheaply made and often discarded. For instance, there were many coronation souvenirs which contained advertising messages from manufacturers such as Cadbury, Rowntree, and Oxo. They were often in the form of biscuit tins or sweet tins. Offbeat items such as a 1953 coronation kite, a plastic doll in the form of Queen Elizabeth, or even a coronation bottle opener, can be of interest to collectors, though prices are seldom high.

And finally, on the subject of bottles, there have been several special ales brewed to commemorate royal events. Often you see them advertised for sale at £100 or more. But it is a myth that coronation ale is either sought after or valuable, and in my experience, most bottles change hands for little more than £20 or £30.

Above an Edward VII coronation plate. Below rear the examples include stoneware commemorating Queen Victoria's Jubilee.

CRESTED CHINA

The term 'crested china' is used to describe a prolific and highly varied range of wares for the souvenir market that were produced from the mid-nineteenth century until World War II. They are characterized by the heraldic crests they bear, denoting the town or institution they served as souvenirs for.

These pieces, often just a couple of inches tall, were produced from about 1860, with the bulk of production in the early years of this century. They are very popular with collectors because they are cheap, take up little room and were made in such an astounding variety. Manufacturers were keen to follow any fad or jump on any bandwagon, and the result has been a positive plethora of crested items.

Crested-ware bathing huts recall the late Victorian period, straw boaters and wind-up gramophones evoke the Edwardian era and the harsh realities of the First World War are reflected in model machine gunners, airships, hand grenades and ambulances. Even the roaring twenties are captured with models of flapper girls.

The man who began the whole crested ware craze was W.H. Goss, who began making these novelty items in the last few decades of the nineteenth century. By 1900 the boom had started; other manufacturers followed his example and soon there was no town in the country without its own crested ware.

Goss specialized in historical items at first, often using Roman relics as models for a range of vases, jugs and urns. The company widened its range later and among the most collected items are the famous Goss cottages. More than forty different ones were produced, the most famous and most common being Anne Hathaway's cottage and Shakespeare's house. Perfect examples of these can now fetch £200 or more. Rarer buildings, such as the Cat and Fiddle Inn at Buxton can fetch a great deal more and some models, for example the Old Smith at Gullane, are so rare that they can fetch as much as £600.

Gossware – it has the name and a phoenix motif on the base – is the most sought after by collectors, and the most expensive, but common items are still available for as little as £5. Other makers, such as Arcadian, Grafton, Carlton, Shelley, Swan and Willow, are of equally good quality but fetch less because they were followers, rather than innovators. Examples of their wares are still available at antiques fairs and shops for as little as £2, allowing plenty of scope for up-and-coming collectors with limited funds.

If collecting crested china appeals to you, then whenever possible go for more unusual items. Crested animals or domestic objects are much more interesting than just vases or jugs, and never buy chipped or cracked examples, as they will never appreciate in value. Military items are among the most collected, and the most expensive. Model tanks, bombs, aeroplanes, war memorials, soldiers, and even the nurse, Edith Cavell, were all modelled and can fetch £20 to £50 each.

Heraldry in miniature. These examples of the souvenir or crested wares of W.H. Goss in 'ivory china' are perhaps the pottery equivalent of postage stamps.

DECANTERS

The first decanters appeared around 1620. These early examples were made without stoppers, the reason being was that the contents were invariably consumed during the meal, so there was no need for an airtight top. In the eighteenth century however, the growing popularity of port changed the situation. As port was improved by decanting and being kept airtight, the stopper became an important part of the decanter and has remained so.

There was another change in the design of English decanters in 1743 – they became thinner and lighter. The reason was that the government, aware that the glass industry was booming, imposed a heavy excise tax on the weight of glass. Manufacturers responded as might be expected – they used less glass. The tax remained in force for about 100 years.

The eighteenth century is regarded as the classic period for decanter design, with engraving, embossing and cut work extensively used. Decanters were often made in pairs, occasionally in sets, but it was not until the Victorian period that they were used in what has probably turned out to be one of their most popular forms, the tantalus. This is a container for the decanter which has a locking lid or bar which prevents the bottles being used without the permission of the key-holder. Tantali were created to prevent the widespread habit of servants taking a quick drink while dusting or cleaning. Most tantali are made in wood, often decorated with brass or silver, and contain three or four matching decanters.

Anyone wondering about the investment value of tantali might like to note that when recently looking through a 1977 antiques magazine, I saw one advertised for sale by a dealer for £70. Today the identical item would cost more than £300.

The value of decanters depends on many factors, notably age and degree of decoration. Irish examples are sought after, though the quality is not really any better than English. Good seventeenth- and eighteenth- century decanters run well into the three-figure price range, and so do some of the better nineteenth-century examples. But many Victorian and Edwardian decanters of attractive design can still be found in antiques shops for well under £50.

You may find some old decanters have whitish stains inside them. This can be removed by filling the decanter with vinegar, leaving it to stand overnight, then using a tissue and a curved piece of wire to wipe off the stains. Sometimes the stoppers in decanters get stuck. Instead of using force, which can cause breakage, try leaving the decanter overnight in your refrigerator. Next morning you will almost always find that the stopper just lifts out.

The Victorian decanter in the foreground is flanked by two differing shapes of Georgian three-ringed examples. On the far right is a Victorian square-sectioned baluster decanter.

DELFT

Much popular confusion surrounds the term 'Delft', not the least of which relates to its value today. Suffice it to say for the moment that much Delftware is relatively worthless.

Simply described, Delft is a variety of tin-glazed earthernware. The Delft with which most people are familiar, that is, a blue and white pottery, was first produced in Delft in Holland during the second quarter of the seventeenth century in imitation of imported Chinese blue and white porcelain. The period of its finest production was from about 1640 and 1740 and at its best bore the closest resemblance to the original of any European porcelain. The Chinese porcelain most frequently imitated was that from the K'ang Hsi dynasty.

The finest Delft of this kind can often be recognized by the use of a finely-painted purple or dark blue outline into which paler colour-washes are added.

Tin-glazed earthenware was produced in England by Flemish potters as early as 1570, first in Norwich and then in London – some fifty years before Delft became famous. The term 'English Delftware' has become synonymous with the tin-glazed wares of the later seventeenth century in the French style or Dutch-Chinese style. However, unlike most of the Continental tin-glazed wares the English examples used only high-temperature colours – blue, green, manganese purple, yellow and a poor red. Stylized fruit and foliage were popular themes in the late seventeenth century.

A Dutch or English charger dating from about 1700 is likely to cost in excess of £1,000. A smaller example of the ware, such as an eighteenth-century plate, can still be found for under £50. A twentieth-century example, often with the word 'Delft' written on the base would be almost worthless.

An eighteenth-century Delft plate and two nineteenth-century vases.

DINKY TOYS

Just over fifty years ago, in a small factory in Liverpool, production began on a series of tiny items which were to become an essential part of childhood in Britain – the Dinky toy. When the first range of cars, vans and lorries rolled off that production line half a century ago, no-one could ever envisage a time when metal toys costing a shilling or two would one day be worth up to £200 or more. But that time has come. For Dinkys are among the most intensely collected toys and are even sold at Sotheby's and Christie's.

Even those who realize that Dinkys are sought after seldom know which ones command the high prices, or why. While age and, of course, condition are vitally important, it is often the advertising logo on the vans or trucks which can boost the price. For example, the Dinky Trojan van, advertising Brooke Bond Tea, is worth perhaps £15 in good condition, but the same van advertising Oxo can top £50. This astonishing difference is simply because some advertisements had 'short run' productions and are rarer.

Some Dinkys were sold in sets and these can fetch a quite staggering amount in pristine condition. A pre-war set of six models – a van, lorry, tractor, tank and two cars – has been sold in auction for £1,300. A complete set of thirteen delivery vans, early models with all-metal wheels, can command as much as £5,000 from a keen collector.

But before you start digging out your childhood relics from the attic, a word of caution. Very high prices come only for models in exceptional condition and which are usually boxed. Cars which have been scratched and battered by boisterous schoolboys are worth very little, though some can be restored by enthusiasts, who are prepared to refit and respray the vehicles in much the same way as full-size cars and vans are renovated.

Generally, Dinky goods vehicles fetch higher prices than cars. For instance, the Dinky Regent petrol tanker made in 1957 is considered rare and usually tops the £100 mark. Sadly, the Dinky toy empire folded in 1979, a victim of intense trading pressure from other manufacturers. But even this has been a bonus to collectors as Dinky prices are gradually forced up as more collectors seek fewer vehicles.

A selection of Dinky toys in pristine condition. Note that vans carrying advertising logos such as 'Heinz' and 'Golden Shred', shown here, frequently fetch high prices.

DOLLS

I was once standing in the office of a well-known auction house when a middle-aged lady came in and placed a small cardboard box on the desk. Carefully she removed the lid and from many folds of tissue paper she took a doll and handed it to the valuer. She said the doll had been in her family for about 100 years and that as she had recently seen an old doll in an antiques shop priced at £50, she wondered if this particular one was worth as much as that.

The valuer examined the doll carefully for a few minutes without saying a word, then finally he spoke. 'I'm afraid your estimate of £50 is not very accurate,' he told her. She looked very disappointed. Then the valuer smiled. 'At auction I think we should get about £2,000 for this doll.' I reached across for a chair for the lady since she looked as though she needed to sit down!

It turned out that the doll was made by the famous French firm, Jumeau, makers of some of the finest quality dolls. It had a bisque (unglazed china) head with a fine, lifelike complexion and superb blue eyes. The doll was dressed in its original clothes – pale green dress with matching bonnet, and even had tiny, hand-made boots with real leather soles. The famous make, excellent condition and the original clothes all combined to make this doll very desirable among collectors, who will pay hundreds, often thousands of pounds for perfect examples of dolls by famous makers.

The doll as a toy dates back thousands of years, but examples earlier than about 1750 are sufficiently scarce to become museum pieces. In the late 1700s wax dolls were made as were papier mâché ones. It was not until the early Victorian period, 1840 onwards, that dolls with china heads were popular. The great heyday of this type of doll was from about 1870 until the First World War. During this period the quality of doll manufacture reached its peak, with firms from Germany and France dominating the market. Thousands of dolls from the continent were imported into Britain. These dolls usually, but not always, had the maker's name or initials stamped on the back of the neck.

Names to look for, apart from Jumeau, are Simon and Halbig, Kammer and Reinhardt from Germany, and Jules Nicholas Steiner, Bru and S.F.B.J. from France. Many dolls were not marked but can be attributed to these firms by experts. While such dolls are very valuable, anonymous makes from the same period are worth much less. Condition and originality are of paramount importance in assessing value.

Dolls with heads made from cloth, simulated china or other substances come much lower down the price scale. Often such dolls date from the inter-war period. Dolls which have musical movements fitted are very sought after, provided they are old, as most musical or talking dolls are of twentieth-century manufacture.

Victorian dolls. The quality of the dresswork is a large determinant in their value.

DOULTON CHARACTER JUGS

Character jugs have been made in Britain since the middle of the eighteenth century and the best known example is the Toby Jug, made popular by the Ralph Wood Company of Burslem in the Staffordshire Potteries. But in pure collecting terms there is no doubt that the most popular character jugs are those made by the Royal Doulton Company. The firm's first character jug, John Barleycorn, was produced in the 1930s and designed by Charles Noke, Doulton's Art Director.

Several other characters were quickly added and all of them proved popular. Since that time dozens of other characters both real and fictional have been added to the range which embraces several different sizes.

The fact that the jugs are well designed, colourful, interesting and take up little shelf space has given them immense collecting appeal, with values linked to rarity. Some characters were produced for only a short period before being withdrawn and these are the ones most eagerly sought by collectors. From time to time the Doulton Company also withdraws certain characters in order to make way for new designs, and these 'out of production' models begin to increase in value as soon as they have been deleted.

Some indication of the tremendous value of withdrawn character jugs can be gained from the following two examples. During the Second World War Doulton produced a Winston Churchill character jug but it was marketed for only a short while before being withdrawn, reputedly because Churchill felt the jug unflattering. Today an example would fetch at least £5,000.

In 1984 the company produced a celebrity jug depicting the film actor Clarke Gable but for reasons never made public the jug was quickly withdrawn and only a few dozen are known to be circulating; collectors are prepared to pay £2,000 to £3,000 to acquire one.

Rarities exist in all sizes of Doulton character jugs. After the first production run minor changes in design or colouring can turn the item into a collector's piece. Finally, a word of caution: there are many Doulton 'seconds' on the market, all containing minor flaws which have caused them to be rejected by the factory quality control inspectors. These are sold off as seconds but to denote that fact the company drills out the centre of its trade mark emblem on the base. This can sometimes be hard to spot and there are some dealers unscrupulous enough to sell these rejects as perfect examples and at full market price. Rejects have little value to the true collector, so be warned.

Although the Royal Doulton factory was initially known for traditional salt-glaze stoneware jugs, in the twentieth century it is their face jugs that have become the vogue.

EGG CUPS

There is some evidence that egg cups were in use in Roman times though they probably date back much further. In Britain though, their widespread use is comparatively recent. Until the eighteenth century eggs were roasted rather than boiled and therefore there was no need for a special cup in which to put the egg.

The boiling of eggs began to catch on in the eighteenth century and by the nineteenth century was very popular. Most early egg cups were finely crafted items, beautifully made in unusual woods such as yew and cherry, or made in silver or porcelain of the highest quality. This was simply because the practice of eating boiled eggs was mostly confined to the wealthy.

By the middle of the nineteenth century the boiled egg had become a regular feature of the Victorian breakfast, and manufacturers were turning out a wide variety of cheaply-made egg cups not only from wood and earthernware, but even material like papier mâché. Many of these egg cups were rather plain but towards the turn of the century there was an increasing trend towards novelty egg cups designed to appeal to children. This trend gathered momentum in the early years of this century and has continued to the present time.

Since most egg cups were turned out by the million to be sold cheaply, and not expected to last too long, they seldom contained manufacturer's markings and therefore difficult to date. Examples from noted firms such as Minton or Doulton can be dated because these did have marks but the vast majority were turned out by semi-anonymous firms in the Staffordshire Potteries.

Collecting egg cups is a growing pastime for many for the items cost so little and take up little space. Most examples are obtainable for just a pound or two but older and more unusual ones fetch a little more. It is surprising just how many designs have been used for egg cups – rabbits, chickens, dogs, bears, elephants, motorcars, trains, tanks, aeroplanes and many human forms – including policemen, clowns and bald-headed men have all been incorporated in egg-cup designs.

Since World War II there have been many egg cups linked to children's television or comic books. The two best known are probably Sooty, and Noddy the Enid Blyton character. More recently Huckleberry Hound, Paddington Bear and characters from the Magic Roundabout series have found their way on to egg cups and are already regarded as collector's items.

Both new and old examples of novelty egg cups, all of them gems for a collector.

ENAMELS

The Black Country is a sprawling industrial landscape between Birmingham and Wolverhampton. There is a small town within this urban patchwork called Bilston and to be quite candid, it is not the sort of place that would find its way onto any tourist's itinerary. Yet it does have one great claim to fame, for Bilston enamels are highly collected and though they were made cheaply as gifts and souvenirs in the eighteenth and nineteenth centuries, examples can now fetch hundreds of pounds each.

Enamel is actually finely powdered glass which is fused by intense heat onto a metal surface, usually copper. The effects can be stunning, with different layers of enamel highly polished and brightly coloured. Enamel work was used to make eye-catching trinkets, especially jewellery, though it is small boxes which are most eagerly sought by collectors these days.

Enamels were originally created by the Egyptians and later by the Chinese, but it was not until about 1600 that they became popular in Europe. The French became the best exponents of the art and by comparison the work from Bilston and Battersea, the other great English centre of enamel work, is quite poor. But because the French Revolution effectively cut off the market for fine enamels, English wares became increasingly sought after.

Each art form produces its own supreme master craftsman and in enamel work it is the name of Fabergé that is hallowed. He specialized in using translucent enamels involving a layer technique which required intense heat. Each layer had to be baked individually. The bases or frameworks for the enamels were mostly engine-turned metals, including gold. Decorative engraving was done by hand. While few people could ever afford an example of Faberge's work, there are more humble but still charming items around. Even so, you are unlikely to get much change out of £100 for a good Victorian example and fine quality work commands much higher sums.

An enamelled bottle c. 1900, a Japanese cloisonné napkin ring and a Battersea enamel box.

ETCHINGS

In the days before photography the only way for most people to find out what places, famous people, or rare plants and animals were like was to study prints. Etchings are one form of print and they were very fashionable and popular in the eighteenth and nineteenth centuries.

Most prints were made from line engravings on copper or steel plates and were often inaccurate because they were the work of several craftsmen. The artist who did the original work might never see the finished print; it might also pass through the hands of a number of designers and engravers and subtle alterations could take place. Etchings have a special quality, however, because they were almost always the work of the artist himself and retain more accuracy of detail and feeling of spontaneity.

Etchings are made by covering a metal plate with a thin coating of wax. The picture is then 'drawn' on the wax by the artist using a needle-like tool. The plate is then immersed in a bath of acid which does not attack the wax, but bites into the exposed areas of the metal plate. Tonal quality is achieved by removing the plate from the acid, varnishing some of the lines and then re-immersing. This process can take place several times before the etching is finished.

While primitive forms of etching were known as early as the sixteenth century, its greatest exponent in the seventeenth century was Rembrandt. It was not until 100 years later that it became popular in Britain. The two best known English etchers are Francis Barlow and Francis Place. In the eighteenth century Hogarth, Gainsborough and Paul Sandby all produced etchings and one of the best known exponents was Thomas Rowlandson.

The best-known etcher of Victorian times was probably Samuel Palmer, the great painter who turned to etching in later life. His attention to detail, involving the master plates being reworked time and time again, has not been surpassed.

While examples by famous etchers fetch good prices, there are many fine etchings by other craftsmen still available in antique shops and auctions for just a few pounds.

A craft in its own right, etching is no less creative than painting.

FAIRINGS

If you visited a fairground during the nineteenth century, it would be unlikely you would come away without having bought, or perhaps won, a fairing. Small ornaments, usually featuring a comic domestic situation, they were a sort of ceramic version of the seaside postcard.

Made as small figure groups, they appear to represent a pure strand of British humour, yet surprisingly they were mostly made in Germany. They were extremely popular in Britain between about 1860 and the turn of the century, although their quality deteriorated substantially after the first few years of production.

Many depicted newlyweds or drunken husbands and frequently carried a small caption, one of the most common of which read, 'Last to bed to put out the light'. Another, 'Returning at one o'clock in the morning', was also very popular.

Mass-produced fairings were manufactured by one company, Conta & Boehme of Pössneck. The inscriptions on these fairings were always in English but the lettering has a Teutonic flavour. Around the turn of the century, rival firms in Saxony began flooding the market with inferior examples, undercutting Conta & Boehme. These examples are easily recognized by their gaudiness and their excessive use of gilding. They were also hollow, being made from mechanical moulds and lacked the bases of earlier, better examples. Many of them also have 'Made in Germany' imprinted on them. Examples of fairings were also imported into Britain from Japan.

All fairings are collected, but enthusiasts prefer the early models when the quality and detail were much better.

These comic vignettes are typical of nineteenth-century fairings, exhibiting a style of humour later found on seaside postcards.

O do leave me a drop

FANS

It was one of those occasions when Queen Victoria was not amused. The year was 1870, and Victorian fashion was at the height of ostentation. Long, elegant dresses, with bustles and frills, ornate, wide-brimmed hats, dainty parasols. And for those special dinner parties and dances, one essential fashion accessory – a fan.

What did not amuse the Queen was the fact that the fans being widely used were not made in Britain – they were all imported. Accordingly, the Queen decided to try to revive the dying craft of fan making in this country by offering a prize of £400 – a small fortune at the time – for the best-designed fan, at a special exhibition she arranged. While the event attracted much attention, it did not achieve its objective, for fans were in such a decline they were to become virtually extinct by the turn of the century.

Fans, in primitive form, date back to Biblical times, when they were literally large palm leaves used for cooling oneself on hot days. But in the Middle Ages in Europe they were being used as decorative fashion accessories, though they were frequently a means of concealing the rotten teeth of ladies living in those rather unhygienic times! Beautiful women with blackened molars would peer alluringly over the tops of pretty, colourful fans, hoping to attract male attention without revealing their toothy short-comings!

It was in the seventeenth and eighteenth centuries that the manufacture of fans reached a peak, and surviving examples from this period can fetch several hundred pounds from keen collectors. The best fans, with intricate design and construction, were made in France and Italy.

The functional part of the fan is called the leaf, and can be made from a wide variety of materials, such as paper, net, parchment, silk or crepe. The arm of the fan, known as the stick, can be made from wood, ivory, mother-of-pearl or tortoiseshell. The fanmakers' art often reached quite breath-taking proportions. Fans were carved, pierced, decorated with silver and precious stones, and often hand-painted.

By the Victorian era, the role of the fan had been reduced to a mere fashion accessory, carried like a purse or evening bag, but seldom used.

These days, it is only Victorian fans which are within the scope of collectors, and even some of these examples can fetch large sums if very pretty. Most nineteenth-century fans were French or Spanish origin. French examples, often enhanced with water-colour scenes, are the more collectable, as Spanish varieties were generally of poorer quality.

By the Edwardian era, changing social habits had signalled the end for the fan, though their use lingered on into the 1920s on a small scale.

A selection of painted parchment, wood and parchment/wood fans. Black fans, simply decorated, were often used as mourning fans by the Victorians.

FIREMARKS

If you have ever seen a strange-looking plaque high up on the wall of a building bearing just a symbol, you may well have been mystified by its purpose. Chances are it was probably a firemark and some of these plaques are now so valuable that villains have been known to shin up ladders in the dead of night to prise them loose. Most are worth more than £50 each and a few can even top £1,000.

Firemarks were introduced in the late seventeenth century as a means of indicating whether a house was insured. In those days there was no national fire brigade service. Insurance companies ran their own fire brigades and if your house caught fire and was not insured, it would just burn to the ground, often watched by fire fighters from the insurance company who would be remarking on just how important it was to be insured.

Firemarks were applied to insured buildings and each insurance company had its own distinctive symbol. The mark had to be easily recognized, for the firemen were mostly illiterate. When fire broke out, several brigades would answer the call. If the first brigade was not the one from the right insurance company, they were supposed to put out the fire and be later reimbursed by the insurance company concerned. Often, though, the firemen, not seeing 'their' symbol on the house, would merely warm their hands by the blaze and not lift a finger to put it out.

Early firemarks were made of lead, but later examples were made from copper, tin and cast iron. They stayed in use until the middle of the nineteenth century, when local councils took over responsibility for firefighting. Some were in use until about 1900, but only for advertising purposes. Genuine firemarks make interesting collections and good investments, but steps should be taken to ensure authenticity before parting with a sum of money, for there are many fakes in this field. Cast iron and lead firemarks are easily cast and easily aged almost overnight and there are a large number in circulation which look very authentic.

Many other mementos of fire brigades are now being collected; brass fireman's helmets, for instance, and even complete uniforms. Badges and belts are in demand, and even the fire engines themselves. Competition to collect these sorts of items is certainly increasing.

The right to enjoy the services of the fire brigade no longer depends on having one of these attached to your wall. Nevertheless they are highly desirable objects and widely collected.

FISHING TACKLE

There are people who think anglers are a little eccentric. They set off, frequently at dawn, to travel miles away, merely to stand about on cold, damp, dismal river banks. And for what? To spend hours trying to catch fish which they often then put back into the water.

What about those who collect old fishing tackle which they have no intention of ever using? Obsolete rods and reels can now be worth big money to keen collectors whose interest in fishing is often academic. You won't find them catching a chill on some remote river bank. They prefer to stay at home, occasionally polishing an old brass fishing reel, or merely musing in an armchair by the fire, surrounded by ancient fishing rods which may not have been used for more than half a century. And if you think such collectors are few and far between, then think again.

The demand for old fishing tackle is so great that many of the country's top auctioneers stage regular sales devoted purely to old angling equipment. Not only do rods and reels come under the auctioneer's hammer, but flies, gaffs, landing nets and sundry other bits and bobs.

Fishing reels attract particular attention and while common examples fetch £30 or £40, some rarities can make as much as £300. In this class comes the Hardy 'Perfect' brass salmon fly reel, made about 1894. Another Hardy model which can top £200 was their Bougle trout fly reel made about 1912. The Bougle, named after its French inventor, was an especially light reel which could take a lot of line, but only a few were made, hence the price.

Even fishing literature has a market; not only books on angling, but old catalogues and advertising material, and certainly prints and paintings. But before you clamber into the attic in search of grandfather's fishing tackle, a word of caution. High prices are only obtained for rarities, usually more than fifty years old and often as much as a hundred years old. Mostly they have makers' names which are of special interest to collectors. In fact, you could say they are the reel thing.

Reels, rods and even early line are all collected. Particularly valued are collections of early flies.

GLASS PAPERWEIGHTS

If you stood six feet away from a table on which were two glass paperweights, one brand new and costing 75 pence from a department store and the other made about 1850 and worth perhaps £5,000, it is doubtful is you could tell the difference, but on much closer examination even the inexperienced eye could discern the fine detail of the antique example.

Glass paperweights appear to have been first made about 1845 and the most popular form was a glass ball with brightly coloured flowers trapped inside. Other versions featured butterflies, insects, tiny snakes and reptiles, or even portraits. These paperweights, often known as 'millefiore' meaning 'thousand flowers', were made in France, England and America and collectors feel that early French examples are the best.

It was not until 1851, the year of the Great Exhibition, that this type of paperweight became popular. Until then they had been looked on as novelties. Now collectors regard them as miniature works of art and early ones can fetch thousands of pounds at auction.

Apart from the sheer quality and detail of antique paperweights, another way of telling if they are genuine is to examine the flat base. Most old ones have a rough, often jagged, spot in the centre called the pontil or punty mark. This mark was made by the glassmaker's pontil rod being broken from the finished article and such a mark occurs on many pieces of old glassware.

Early glass paperweights, particularly ones from the Clichy and Baccarat areas of France are now so expensive to buy that only wealthy collectors can indulge. But there is still scope for the collector of more limited means. While not so attractive as floral examples, the souvenir glass paperweight offers a great deal of fascination, and some Victorian examples can cost as little as a few pounds. These were produced from 1850 onwards and are in the form of a glass blob or dome which acts as a magnifying glass for a coloured or sepia print which is stuck to the underside. These prints usually feature town or seaside views and are, in effect, a tiny window to the past, showing holiday resorts and street scenes as they were more than 100 years ago. Changes in clothes, social customs, and transport can be clearly observed.

Prior to about 1870 this type of paperweight was mostly circular, but following this period they became more adventurous in design and were even produced in the shape of hearts and horseshoes.

Another type to look out for is a paperweight in the form of a slab or plaque of white china with an embossed design, the whole thing set in glass. Made by Aspley Pellatt of the Falcon Glassworks in Southwark, they were produced between 1820 and 1850 by him, and later by other manufacturers. Despite mass production, examples are rare and no collection is complete without one.

A selection of inexpensive paperweights, one backed with a scenic photograph and two millefiori examples.

GLASSWARE

Glass was first made as early as 1500 BC, was perfected by the Romans and brought to new heights of splendour by the Venetians between the thirteenth and seventeenth centuries.

Early examples of English and European glass are only for the fairly wealthy collector. But most of the glassware you will see at antiques fairs and in shops is likely to be no older than Victorian, not really rare, and not terribly expensive.

The most common of all glass is pressed ware, which was introduced in this country around 1840. Items were pressed out of moulds and this method was used to mass produce a vast amount of domestic ware. Strong and robust, large quantities have survived and examples are so common they can be almost worthless.

Quality is the factor that makes glass valuable and it is important to be able to tell the difference between pressed glass and cut glass. Many people think that any patterned glass must be cut, but even a century ago mass produced pressed glass was so sophisticated it can deceive all but the most experienced eye. A simple way to tell the difference is to hold the item in a strong light and look closely at the patterned edges. Genuine cut glass will have sharply defined, razor-like edges to the pattern. Moulded or pressed examples will show a much blunter definition.

Wine glasses and decanters are probably the most appreciated by collectors and the finest examples were made in the eighteenth century, though it was the nineteenth century that saw glassware manufactured on the greatest scale. Ruby or cranberry – glass with a red or pink tint – was popular and other types include vaseline glass (green or yellow) and carnival glass (orange or purple).

Slag glass is also popular. This type is also known as 'end of the day' glass, because it is made from the molten waste in blast furnaces which was skimmed off at the end of shifts. It can be very pretty and has a veined appearance, like marble. Nailsea glass – made in many places, not just near Bristol – is another example of beautiful colouring, usually in a looped or waved formation of contrasting colours.

Decoration on glass can be cut with a metal or stone wheel, engraved or etched with acids, or even embellished with air bubbles, often called tears.

The scope for collecting glass is enormous, but however pretty a piece may be, make sure you examine it closely before buying, as the slightest crack or chip will devalue it considerably. Remember also, that dating glass can be difficult because it exhibits little signs of wear and was seldom marked by manufacturers.

A selection of glassware. Centre top is a nineteenth-century cranberry-glass claret jug. Below centre is a Victorian epèrre.

GRAMOPHONES

Whilst it was Thomas Edison who gave us the wax-cylinder phonograph (listed separately in this volume) the credit for inventing the flat disc gramophones goes to Emile Berliner, a German-born American.

It was 1887, ten years after Edison patented his phonograph, that Berliner devised his flat disc machine which used an improved recording technique to produce greater sound clarity. The gramophone quickly became popular, initially as a children's toy using nursery rhyme records, but within a short time its wider potential was appreciated and many manufacturers began production. Early models were hand driven, with the first spring driven models introduced in 1896. From that time onwards the gramophone quickly ousted its rival phonograph and established the foundation on which today's modern recording industry is based.

During the early years of this century gramophones had large external horns but these were soon replaced by machines with internal horns and lidded cabinets.

There is growing interest in all gramophones, which for many years were overshadowed by musical boxes and phonographs. The most desirable gramophone is probably the one known as the 'dog' model, introduced in 1898 and the one used as the trade mark, along with Nipper the dog, by the His Master's Voice Company. Examples are rare and fetch more than £1,000.

Typical Edwardian horn gramophones are becoming increasingly scarce and novice collectors frequently have to make do with later, internal horn machines. Wooden table models with lift-up lids and small portable gramphones looking like attaché cases, are still fairly common, though rising in price, and there is eager demand for children's or novelty machines. For instance the Mikiphone, a pocket-sized gramophone made in the 1920s attracts great attention, along with various types of camera-phone, which looked rather like folding Kodak cameras from the same period.

Among the more unusual, if not eccentric, gramophones was the German Stollwereck model made at the turn of the century. It was designed for use with chocolate discs, so that if you didn't like the tune you could always eat the record!

Early gramophones. The large, brass-horned example is an American Victor c. 1910. Left, an HMV portable, mid-1920s, and a German Nirona portable c. 1925.

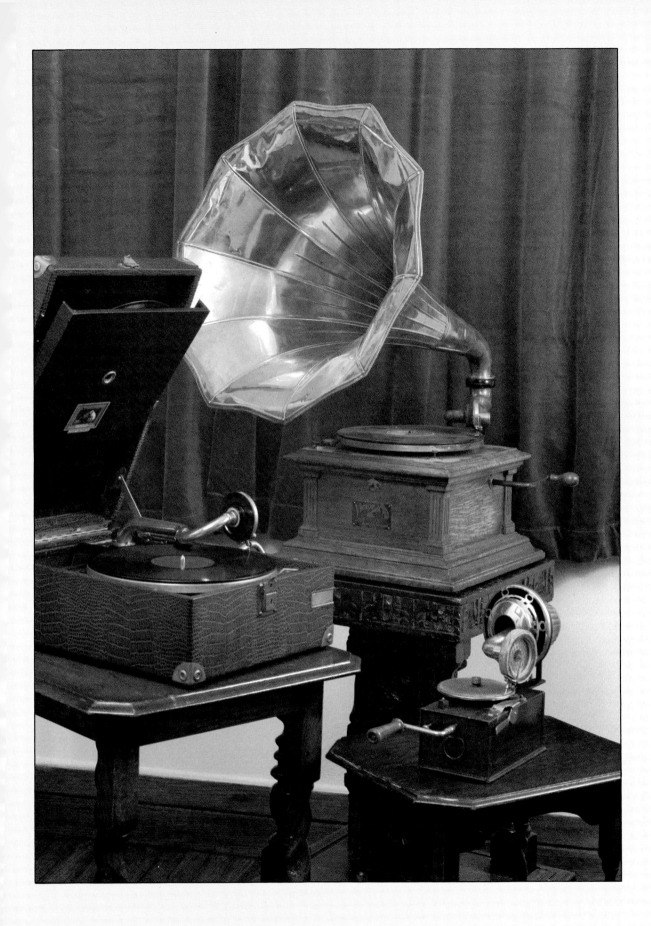

GRAMOPHONE RECORDS

Old gramophone records – those highly breakable 78s used on wind-up gramophones – seem to have survived in vast numbers. I am frequently asked if these records are of any value. Well, yes and no.

Ninety percent of all 78s are worth no more than a few pence each, if you can get even that for them, but the remaining 10 percent can be worth several pounds each to certain collectors. On the whole, records featuring opera, classical or light orchestral music are virtually worthless, irrespective of which musicians are involved. These discs are simply not in demand and most antiques dealers who come across them have to virtually give them away.

Certain individual musicians are collected in their own right, as are outstanding classical singers such as Caruso, Clara Butt, Nellie Melba and others, and in terms of value only their early work is collected because there were so many re-issues. 'Early' in record terms usually means pre-1905 for it was then that the double-sided record came into production. From about 1898 to 1905 gramophone records had a track on one side only. These single-sided records are of value only if the featured artist is collected. Military bands and the church choirs were frequently recorded and few want to collect this sort of record.

The period from 1920 to 1950 was the great heyday of the 78 record and the most collected records from this era are the 'big band' sounds. Top bands led by such great names as Geraldo, Ambrose, Jack Payne and others still have a keen following and recordings by them in excellent condition can be worth a pound or more to enthusiasts.

Celebrity entertainers such as George Formby, Gracie Fields, and even Max Miller attract collectors and their records, too, have higher than average value.

Disposing of unwanted 78s can be difficult, as many antiques dealers don't bother with them. You have to locate a collector, either by advertising or by going to an antiques fair where a specialist dealer may be present.

Scratches notwithstanding, many 78s are almost obsessively collected by enthusiasts.

HATPINS

Collecting hatpins is the sort of hobby that can easily go to your head. One enthusiast has paid two thousand pounds for a single hatpin, which certainly proves the point. Granny's old hatpins are not, of course, all worth that sort of money, but many are worth a few pounds each if they have a pretty, decorative head.

Hatpins really had their heyday about a 100 years ago. If you study photographs of Victorian ladies, you will see that long hair was the fashion and often it was worn in a bun or coiled form. This provided a good base that could be used to pin the elaborate, wide-brimmed hats which were also in fashion at the time.

The hatpin itself became an important dress accessory on a par with brooches, lockets or rings. Hatpin makers went to extraordinary lengths to attract buyers with beautiful creations. Hatpins were made with a wide variety of decorative heads, using glass, china, pearl, silver, jade, jet, semi-precious stones and, on occasions, gold and diamonds. They were in such constant use that they created a spin-off industry for hatpin cases, boxes, trays or holders. The humble hatpin also came with matching accessories, such as buckles and buttons. Themes were often reflected in the heads of the hatpins. If they were going to watch a hockey match, or a game of tennis, ladies might well wear a hatpin featuring a hockey stick or a tennis raquet.

The length of hatpins varies, from just a couple of inches to more than a foot. These long pins were considered dangerous if they projected too far through the hat, and some ladies wore small, decorative protectors over the sharp point in order to avoid piercing a passer-by.

Collecting hatpins is a growing hobby, possibly because the pins are relatively cheap and take up little storage space. Many who collect pins mount them on velvet or other suitable material and either display them in frames or small cabinets.

There are almost as many ornamental heads for hatpins as there are pins themselves. Elaborate, classical jewelled heads gave way to novelty pins towards the end of the nineteenth century.

HORSE BRASSES

Of all the forms of brassware, the most popular among collectors is probably horse brasses, yet few people know that horse brasses have been made in Britain for 2,000 years. These decorative items have associations with mystic cults, sorcery and witchcraft and the origin of the designs of many horse brasses lie in lucky symbols, said to ward off evil spirits.

A few hand-made Georgian period brasses, mostly made between 1750 and 1800, are still available, but almost all the horse brasses that turn up in antique shops are Victorian. Those that are genuine, that is, for many on sale are reproductions or fakes.

The popularity of horse brasses is such that demand far outstrips supply and as they are easy to cast and copy, the market is flooded with new brasses. Sadly, many have been aged with acid to be passed off as the genuine article. Detecting the fakes is not too difficult once you have studied a few genuine examples. Really authentic brasses have a smooth, worn look and a mellow colour which the fakers find hard to duplicate.

From about 1860 onwards, horse brasses were cast in large numbers, filed and drilled by hand and then polished. There was a large demand, since no self-respecting tradesman would take out his horse and cart without a show of brasses on the harness. These days, brasses are used mostly for interior decoration, hung on the walls of pubs and cottages.

There are many different designs, some of them with special meanings. For example, the acorn is a lucky symbol for farmers; the bell will frighten away evil spirits, while the crescent is the symbol of the moon goddess, who would also protect against evil. An endless knot was originally a Buddhist good luck sign, as was a fish. Churns are associated with dairymen, the barrel with breweries. The anchor is a motif of St Nicholas. The star has its origins in ancient mystic religions.

Some symbols are particular to an area or county; the bear, for instance, is associated with Lincolnshire, the sun and the heart with Warwickshire. Collectors are eager to acquire certain symbols such as a railway engine, for this means that the brasses were made especially for horses used by railway companies.

The value of old horse brasses does vary a great deal. Routine late Victorian examples will cost £5 or less. Early, less common types can cost £20 or £30 and straps containing several can cost a great deal more, depending on which varieties are included.

Talismans in brass. Traditional symbols of magical power used on horsebrasses have given way in more recent times to simply ornamental motifs.

IRONS

For most people ironing seems to be the least popular domestic chore and the iron itself seems to have been a symbol of drudgery since its beginnings in the sixteenth century. The idea of an iron may well date back much further but it was around that time that it came into use in Europe and it was the Dutch who pioneered the iron's popularity.

There are two types of iron, the 'hot box' variety which requires hot material being placed inside it, and the more basic solid flat iron which has to be heated on a stove or fire. The use of the iron was well established in Britain when Isaac Wilkinson from Denbighshire took out the first patent for a box iron in this country in 1738. His design was simple and effective and continued to be used for the next two centuries.

Even world wide there was little change in iron design until towards the end of the nineteenth century. Then, the box iron, which required a hot metal slug to be placed into it, declined as other irons which could be filled with hot charcoal or embers increased in popularity. Gas irons were introduced in America in the 1850s and in Britain not long after.

It is surprising to learn that the electric iron was patented as early as 1883 in America though it was a cordless type which was charged with electricity by being placed on a special stand. There have also been irons powered by paraffin, petrol, methylated spirit and even acetylene. In addition to domestic irons there have been irons made for special trades such as tailoring, hat making and even for ironing the cloth on snooker and billiard tables.

The collecting scope for irons is quite enormous and clearly it is the unusual types which collectors seek, though even the rarest types are not tremendously valuable. The most common example which can be found quite easily at antiques fairs or shops is the basic household flat iron, yet even this humble tool comes in a bewildering variety of designs. These flat irons can still be acquired for as little as two or three pounds, often to be used as door stops or unusual paper weights. They do tend to rust and while many people choose to paint them black I prefer to see them wire brushed and then buffed up using traditional black lead. The shiny finish is much more pleasing and surprisingly long lasting.

The traditional flat iron comes in a variety of pleasing and substantial forms and are inexpensive.

JELLY MOULDS

Moulds have been in use for presenting food in a decorative manner since medieval times but it was not until the middle of the last century that they came into widespread use. Before that time moulds had been used almost exclusively by the upper and middle classes for various kinds of puddings and savoury dishes but the Crystal Palace Exhibition of 1851 introduced jelly to the hundreds of thousands of visitors and it was an instant success. This new cheap and easy to make dessert was in such demand that manufacturers produced an endless variety.

Moulds were made from metal, many were earthenware and many more were made from copper. It was copper moulds which tended to be the most decorative and some were made in remarkable forms. All had to have a tin lining as food or liquid heated in copper can be poisonous.

The Victorian copper jelly mould has become a classic kitchen collectable and attractive examples can fetch between £50 and £100. There are many reproductions and outright fakes circulating and these are normally lighter in weight than an original, the design features are not so crisply pressed, and the surface patina is not so mellow. Earthenware moulds are more common and cheaper, with their decorative qualities usually reserved for the interior. While the majority of these moulds have merely a fluted design, perhaps topped with an embossed flower or emblem, some were much more inventive. One example I have seen took the form of a crouched lion.

Demands for moulds made the glass or from tin are in less demand as they are not so visually appealing, but it is worth looking out for moulds which are hinged; these were normally used for special puddings and for chocolate.

Many Victorian jelly moulds are superb sculptured items in their own right.

CORN FLOUR BLANC MANGE
BROWN & POLSON'S

2½ oz (5 table spoonfuls filled level) Corn Flour
2 Pints (3 breakfast cups quite full) good sweet
Mix Corn Flour well with a little of the milk
Heat the rest of the milk to boiling point
Pour Corn Flour into heated milk, stirring well
Add half a teaspoonful of butter
Boil and stir well for 10 minutes (by the clock)
Sugar and flavour, if desired, mixed with
jam or marmalade is
Pour into this mould, a
Re-heat gently, in m
Then turn out and

KITCHEN COLLECTABLES

The nineteenth century transformed eating habits. The growth of the shipping industry, the advent of railways and breakthroughs such as the use of refrigeration allowed the British to sample a much wider range of food. As a result the preparation and presentation of food became more sophisticated.

Not surprisingly manufacturers were quick to catch on to these changes and a bewildering variety of kitchen utensils and devices were manufactured. Some of them, such as pip extractors, knife polishers, apple corers, sugar nippers, vegetable slicers and even marmalade cutters were complicated gadgets which frequently became obsolete in a very short time as more efficient models became available. All this primitive gadgetry is now collected, as are the more practical items from the Victorian kitchen, such as saucepans, spice containers, coffee grinders, ladles, scales, rolling pins and cutlery. The more unusual and the better the condition, the greater the value.

With the trend towards natural foods and a more healthy diet, there is increasing interest in kitchen collectables. Some are bought purely to add decoration and a homely quality to modern kitchens which are often rather clinical. But I know many people who buy relics from the Victorian kitchen for entirely practical reasons – they intend to make use of them. Jam pans, coffee grinders, storage jars, rolling pins, pastry cutters, saucepans, plates, tureens, ladles, graters are all just as useful today as they were 100 years ago.

While many old kitchen items are available quite readily for just a few pounds, there are some which are now so collected they fetch substantial prices. Jelly moulds and corkscrews are two examples and both are dealt with separately in this book.

Many items of Victorian and Edwardian kitchenware have not been reproduced since and will be of value not only to the collector but to the imaginative cook.

LEAD SOLDIERS

Model soldiers were found in Egyptian tombs, but it was not until the seventeenth century that they really became popular in Europe. It was then fashionable to have your own model army and stage your own battles, though such activities were confined to those who were rich. In the eighteenth century model soldiers became everyday playthings, when a Frenchman devised a method of making the tiny figures in the round, rather than the traditional flatback, design.

In this country it was as late as 1890 before lead soldiers became common-place. Then, a toymaker called William Britain, who had previously made clockwork models, invented a method of making hollow lead soldiers, thus reducing manufacturing costs. At first they sold only slowly, but when the London store Gammages began stocking them, they became popular.

By 1902 Britain's company had no fewer than 104 different sets on the market. The company prided itself on the accuracy of the uniforms and the colours of the regiments, but mistakes were sometimes made and sets with errors can fetch very high prices. For example, in 1899 the company issued a set of the King's Royal Rifle Corps wearing spiked helmets, but the troops should have been wearing flat caps. The mistake was quickly rectified, but the spiked helmet men are now much prized by collectors.

The value of lead soldiers is linked very closely to their condition. Battered, scratched examples are virtually worthless, but complete sets, preferably in the original boxes, usually fetch a minimum of £50 and often much more. Rare sets can fetch breathtaking amounts. A Britain's set of Boer War troops sold for £900 not long ago. Fairly common sets however, can be bought for £50 to £100.

Dating sets can be tricky and after 1900 Britain's – the most collected of all makers – embossed their name on most of their output. After 1906 the firm stood its figures on square or rectangular bases. Prior to that, the soldiers had been made on round or oval platforms.

Boxed sets of lead toys soldiers c. 1916, including Scots Guards and French Infantrymen.

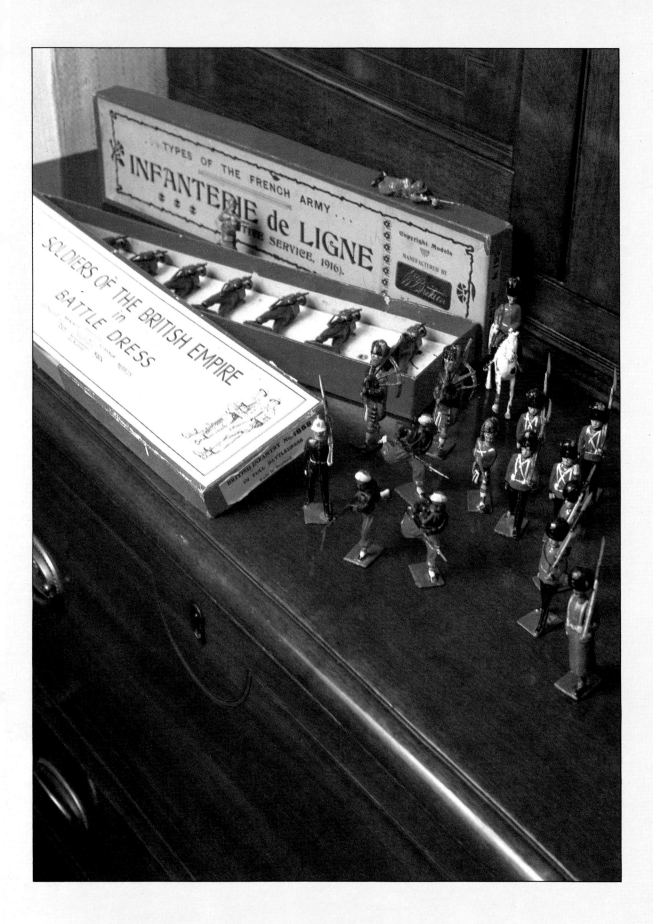

LONGCASE CLOCKS

The longcase clock – it did not become known as the grandfather clock until Victorian times – was first made in the mid-seventeenth century. Although the theory for such clocks had been worked out in the fifteenth century by Leonardo da Vinci, it was not put into practise until some 200 years later and then, by a Dutchman.

The concept quickly caught on in England and early examples were finished in oak with very little decoration. By the William and Mary period (1688–1702), the longcase clock was becoming more decorative. Walnut veneers were used and marquetry and lacquerwork became a common feature.

From about 1720 mahogany veneer cases appeared and further embellishment of the hood took place, with the use of more intricate pediments, turnings and finials. Until this time, most longcase clock faces had been made of brass, but painted dials were becoming popular and the 'moon dial' feature soon followed. This consisted of a rotating pictorial section which was viewed through a 'window' in the main dial, and showed the phases of the moon and often the day of the month.

The early years of the nineteenth century were something of a golden age for quality clock making, with high levels of craftsmanship and design being displayed. But from about 1830 onwards longcase clocks declined in all respects and most Victorian examples tend to be of only average quality, though they often look rather splendid.

While age and design are key factors in valuing longcase clocks, it is undoubtedly the maker who has the most significant effect on the price. While examples from the great master clockmen such as Thomas Tompion, George Graham, Joseph Knibb, and others can fetch a small fortune, many other clockmakers who inscribed their names on the dials of their creations were merely competent craftsmen and do not have such heady appeal. And it must be said that in Victorian times the name that appeared on many painted dial clocks was not actually the maker, but the retailer, who added his name, and that of the town where he traded, to the face of a clock he would have bought in from London or Birmingham, and which had been manufactured on a large scale.

These days, many fine grandfather clocks, particularly those from the eighteenth and early nineteenth centuries, now command thousands of pounds and even the average Victorian offerings can fetch several hundred pounds. Longcase clock prices seemed to peak in the late 1970s, then declined and have since levelled out. It is still possible to acquire a rather undistinguished Victorian example for as little as £350, though prices are beginning to creep up again. These comparatively low prices relate to painted dial clocks. Brass-faced examples are more eagerly sought after and therefore have a higher value.

An eighteenth-century English longcase clock with a moon dial.
The case is of oak.

MAGIC LANTERNS

Before video, or television, or even before silent movies, there was still a form of screen entertainment which was enjoyed by millions. And it was all thanks to the magic lantern.

Primitive forms of slide projectors, amazingly, date back to around 1650, though in the form that we recognize them today, they peaked in popularity in the last century. Then, powered by gas burners, they were used to put on slide shows in public halls. The slides were usually scenic, as most people in those days had not travelled far in Britain, let alone abroad. But there were also slides which in series form told stories, as well as ones which were comical and cartoon-like. Touring magic lantern shows visited remote country areas staging shows in village halls and the novelty of the magic lantern assured a good crowd, who paid perhaps a penny or so for admission.

Magic lanterns were mostly metal-cased with an extending brass lens. The slides were often put in one by one by hand. The later, more sophisticated models had semi-automatic loading. Smaller models were made for home use, though it was really only the wealthy who could afford to buy them.

The slides were made of glass, often hand-coloured, and the imagination of the artist was such that quite breath-taking special effects could be achieved. I can recall seeing one slide show which started with a lighthouse at sunrise, surrounded by a calm sea, and gradually changed to a night-time storm, with a raging sea and a shipwreck, yet the whole effect of movement was achieved by slow interphasing of still-life slides, without any use of animation.

Many magic lanterns still survive, though most of them over the years have been converted to electric power. They turn up in antique shops, costing from £75 upwards, though rare models by noted makers can fetch several hundred pounds. Slides, too, are still plentiful, with small sets costing just a few pounds.

Interest is growing in the art of the magic lantern and at least one group is travelling the country, still putting on old-fashioned public shows and managing to make a living.

A Victorian magic lantern. Many examples can, of course, still be used today.

MAPS

Old maps often turn up when families have a clearout and many people think that because a map may be a 100 years old, or even more, it is bound to be valuable. Sadly, this is not the case. For maps to be really worth something, they have to date back much further than the last century. Most of the really sought-after maps are from the seventeenth century and by famous cartographers such as John Speed, Philip Lea and Timothy Pont.

Not surprisingly, map-making was a world-wide industry and some of the best known map makers come from far afield. In Europe the Italians, Dutch, French and Germans were among the earliest map makers, but the British had their own pioneers. All these early maps are purely for the specialist collector. Most fetch hundreds of pounds, some thousands.

The maps that most people seem to come across are more recent and are mostly Victorian. They crop up in three main varieties: maps showing the whole of Britain, maps showing counties, and local maps which show particular districts. All these were made in fairly large numbers and are not particularly valuable. Routine nineteenth-century maps can be bought for as little as £5, though framed examples will fetch more.

Maps made for special purposes, such as to show railway lines or canals, have special collectors' value, as so do maps made for the armed forces. This is because while towns, hills and rivers tend to stay put over the years, railway lines and canals can vanish, so old maps which show their original courses are more important. Ordnance survey maps are also beginning to be collected these days. As yet, these maps are of little value, but with the growing interest in the changing countryside, and with many old landmarks disappearing, interest in such maps will continue to grow.

Many maps, especially those showing English counties, and bearing dates as early as the 1600s, have been widely reproduced.

The interest in relatively recent maps, as those here, lies in their ability to show features which may now have disappeared from the landscape.

MEDALS

The most famous medal is undoubtedly the Victoria Cross and on the rare occasions when an example comes up for sale, it can fetch more than £50,000.

Of course, lesser medals can still be of great interest to collectors, though values can vary greatly. Basically, there are three classes of medals. There are bravery awards, such as the Victoria Cross, George Cross, Military Cross, and Distinguished Service Order. Then there are decorations, such as the Order of the Garter, given mostly to high-ranking officers and diplomats, and finally there are campaign medals, given not for a specific act, but for men serving in particular campaigns. It is these campaign medals which attract the largest number of collectors, though the value of such medals is far less than the heady sums achieved by VCs.

Most campaign medals sought by collectors come from the nineteenth century, from conflicts such as the Crimean and the Boer Wars. Within these wars, certain medals have special collectors' appeal, such as those from the famous Rorke's Drift Zulu battle. Victorian campaign medals can range in price from £20 to £2,000, depending upon scarcity.

Medals from World War I are now becoming increasingly collected, but are not yet very valuable. A set of three of the most common Great War medals issued to almost every serving man still commands less than £20 a set. World War II medals are virtually worthless unless in the Bravery or Special Campaign class. For example the Navy General Service Medal is very common and worth around £30, but if it has the bar for the 1949 Yangtze River incident, then its value will be ten times as great.

Until World War II, Britain was the only country to inscribe the name of the recipient and his rank and regiment or ship onto medals. This is important because collectors are interested in the man behind the medal. Many of them take the trouble to research him, his family and his war service. But in World War II there were so many men involved and so many services, that the medals given were anonymous. They did not have the name of the man on them, unless it was a special gallantry award. Because they are so anonymous, they are of little interest to collectors.

Foreign medals are much the same. Medals were brought back by troops from Germany and other countries, but these have little value unless they are rare examples.

In the past, medals have mainly been collected by ex-military men, but in the last twenty years collectors have come from right across the board and are often youngsters who were not even born at the time of the last war.

Medals and Orders are legion. Although they can be expensive you don't have to be wealthy to afford these examples.

DONALD MCGILL

Donald McGill is easily the best known comic postcard artist. His work spans more than fifty years and his characters — buxom ladies with hen-pecked husbands in tow and red-nosed drunks in particular — are a symbol of the British on a seaside holiday.

McGill was born in 1875 and began designing postcards in 1904. He was one of the first exponents of the saucy seaside postcard and his work has a freshness and originality which has attracted large numbers of collectors. He had an extremely long career, working right up until the time he died in 1962 and while all his cards are collected, his pre-First World War cards are most in demand, fetching several pounds each.

His drawings became more daring as the years went by. A girl on the beach in 1920 would be showing little more than her ankle. By 1950 McGill's girls were revealing so much, some of his cards aroused great controversy. His captions too were masterpieces of innuendo.

McGill poked fun at the British on holiday in a way which they understood and enjoyed. His parodies were always sympathetic rather than insulting. One of his favourite seaside characters was a red-faced, scowling, outsized woman with a massive bosom and an even more massive bottom. Frequently she would be venting her wrath on an inoffensive, timid and clearly long-suffering husband.

Yet McGill's humour was nothing if not even-handed. He often depicted men as paunchy, red-nosed drunks, loud-mouthed, tactless and rude. And McGill also had a keen eye for beauty. His bathing belles were stunningly curvaceous — and prepared to be cheeky in more ways than one!

McGill's illustrations of British seaside resorts began a trend which continues today.

MICKEY MOUSE

The demand for Mickey Mouse memorabilia has soared since the world's most famous rodent celebrated his fiftieth birthday in 1978. At an auction in 1984 a 41 cm (16 in) tall Mickey Mouse soft toy, produced around 1930, fetched an astonishing £528.

Walt Disney introduced Mickey to the world in 1928 in a silent movie called *Plane Crazy*, but it was his second film later that year, *Steamboat Willie*, that made Mickey an international celebrity. Since then the big-eared, yellow-gloved creature has seldom been off the screen or out of the news and a merchandising industry was created as early as 1930 to cater for the demand for mouse memorabilia.

The Deans Rag Book Company then launched both Mickey and Minnie Mouse dolls, ranging in height from 15 cm (6 in) to 53 cm (21 in). They were an instant success and demand soared throughout the 1930s. By 1939 there were nine different sizes of soft toys, glove puppets and nightdress cases. Any of the items which have survived are now collectors' items and can be worth several hundred pounds.

Walt Disney sold only the doll manufacturing rights to one company. He sold separate rights to other firms to make everything from Mickey Mouse games to radios, toothbrushes and masks. Then came Mickey Mouse wristwatches and I have it on reliable authority that Emperor Hirohito of Japan wears one. A Mickey Mouse tinplate moneybox has been sold at Sotheby's for £750 and most clockwork and tinplate Mickey Mouse toys in good condition do command prices running into hundreds of pounds. Most pre-war items are likely to be far more valuable than their owners might realize and even Mickey souvenirs made as recently as the 1950s can be collectors' items. Mickey may be more than fifty years old, but he shows no signs of losing his popularity.

The mouse that roared. The echoes can now be expensive.

MONEYBOXES

Save cash in a moneybox and you will be ready for that rainy day. Save the moneybox itself and you could be far better off, for old moneyboxes are among the most collected of all mementoes of childhood and some can be worth quite staggering amounts.

Moneyboxes come in a range of designs and while they have existed in various forms for hundreds of years, the great heyday of the moneybox was the Victorian era, when thrift was promoted as one of the great virtues. Children were encouraged to save, and designers stretched their imaginations to come up with attractive and unusual moneyboxes to try to make saving a real pleasure. They were made in tinplate, cast iron, brass, copper, porcelain, pottery, wood, even glass. In addition to being simple boxes, they came as miniature safes, buildings, animals and human figures, even airships and motor cars.

The more unusual the moneybox, the more it is likely to be worth the attention of the collector, and among the most desirable are mechanical moneyboxes. These were mostly imported from America about a hundred years ago and featured bucking horses, hunters shooting bears, circus tricks, dentists pulling teeth, magicians, and even Jonah swallowed by the whale.

All of these boxes were made of cast iron and work by a spring device. A coin was placed in position, a lever pulled, and the coin was projected inside the box as the figures moved. These types are of enormous interest to collectors and some can fetch hundreds of pounds, depending on rarity and condition.

A word of warning however. These money boxes are the subject of one of the biggest con tricks in the antiques world. Thousands of 'Made in Taiwan' copies have been imported into this country and deliberately aged to fool collectors. The boxes leave the Far East with a 'Made in Taiwan' stamp. By the time they reach Britain the mark has been removed, the cast iron box is aged with chemicals and many have even been buried underground for some time to advance the corrosion. Some are so skilfully aged that even antiques dealers are fooled and offer them for sale in good faith.

The fraud is so widespread that I estimate that as many as nine out of ten such boxes which appear in shops, auction rooms and antiques fairs are fakes. These replicas are worth about £20 as novelties. They are often priced at around £150 or more. If you are tempted to buy one of these mechanical moneyboxes, my advice is to get the seller to give you a written guarantee of its authenticity and age. That way, if it turns out to be a fake, you have an excellent chance of getting your money back.

Incidentally, one way to identify a geniune example is to look for its patent date on the base. Fakes do not usually have this information.

A selection of late nineteenth-century moneyboxes including the 'Sambo' moneybox, whose eyes rolled when a coin was dropped into its mouth.

MOTORING MEMORABILIA

Motoring enthusiasts from all over the world will often gather in London salerooms, their pockets bulging with cash and their cheque books at the ready. Yet there may not be a single motor car in sight. These collectors will be caught up in one of the fastest growing areas of the ever-changing world of antiques – automobilia.

They are eager to acquire any relics from a bygone age of motoring and car mascots are among the most sought-after items. In the 1920s and 30s unusual radiator caps were part of a car's character and mascots in the form of birds, dogs, huntsmen, nymphs, or even naked ladies were commonplace.

Fine examples, particularly those associated with quality cars, can fetch anything from £30 to several hundred pounds. Particularly sought are glass mascots made by the French designer, Lalique. Enamel badges from motoring clubs are also popular with collectors, along with early mementoes relating to the AA and the RAC.

Other collectables include motoring trophies, chauffeurs' uniforms, travelling trunks, headlamps, radiator grilles, dashboard instruments, motoring prints, handbooks, and advertising signs.

Enamelled club badges, brassware and mementoes of the AA and RAC are all prized motoring memorabilia.

MOURNING JEWELLERY

The Victorians may have loved life, but they also had a macabre interest in death. This interest was so great that it bordered on enthusiasm and it actually created a special trade – the manufacture of mourning jewellery.

Early in the nineteenth century the 'cult' was already well established, and periods of mourning seemed endless, but it was Queen Victoria herself who took the practice to quite extraordinary lengths.

When her husband, Albert, died suddenly in 1861 after a short marriage, Victoria naturally went into a period of mourning. It lasted forty years, until her death in 1901. As Head of State, her behaviour and beliefs became standard practice for other women and any woman widowed had to go into years of mourning for the late lamented, whether she wanted to or not.

Jewellery makers were quick to see a lucrative market for morbid mementos. Grieving for the dead, could, they felt, have its own fashions and trends. Mourning jewellery took many forms, best known of which are probably brooches made of jet, a coal-like substance, which itself is found at Whitby, Yorkshire. There, a trade which supported hundreds of workers began and lasted almost half a century. Jet was easily carved, cheap to obtain, and the mourning brooches and necklaces it was made into were widely purchased by tearful widows.

These days, jet items are just as widely collected and the carving and decoration on them much admired. Many examples are still available for just a few pounds.

Mourning jewellery was not confined to humble jet; gold and silver were used, and enamel work, cameos, precious stones, all played their part. Hair cut from the head of the deceased was also used, either encased in a brooch as a memento, or woven to form part of the decoration.

Not all mourning items were black. There was a period known as half-mourning which referred to the later period of mourning, when the funeral was several years in the past. At such times discreet shades of grey, or even lavender, mourning jewellery could be worn, without the wearer becoming a social outcast. Lockets, often with the hair or the photograph of the lost loved one, were also common and even mourning rings were made with black enamel work on gold or silver.

Decoration mostly took the form of hearts or crosses though I have, amazingly, seen a skull and crossbones on one piece of mourning wear. The value of these more unusual examples will vary a great deal and will depend largely on the quality of the precious metal and stones involved.

The sombre intentions of mourning jewellery in no way detracts from the exquisite craftsmanship, often executed in gold, enamel or semi-precious stones.

MOVIE MEMORABILIA

Movies, and more specifically movie stars, have attracted interest and adoration from the public from the days of the silent screen days. Movie buffs are among the most knowledgeable and dedicated of all collectors and demand among them for material relating to their idols is intense almost to the point of being cut-throat. Old film stills, posters, portrait photographs and private letters are sought after, along with scrapbooks, press cuttings, autobiographies and personal effects. Price levels are extremely unpredictable, depending on the fame and popularity of the star and the rarity of material relating to them.

Bing Crosby frequently signed autographs. Others, like Robert Donat, rarely signed anything, making material containing their signature all the more desirable.

Nostalgia for particular films also have a bearing on the value of items connected with a particular star. For instance, a poster advertising the Humphrey Bogart film *Casablanca* would fetch several hundred pounds, yet one from a lesser known Bogart film like *The Big Shot* might fetch as little as £50. There is little logic in the price scales of movie memorabilia. At an auction of entertainments material in 1984 a quantity of coats, shoes, gloves and other items worn by Gracie Fields fetched only £130, yet at the same sale a single paper napkin on which Errol Flynn had written his name and address fetched £75.

As a rough rule of thumb, items relating to stars famous in talkies are worth more than those stars from the silent era. There is more interest in Marilyn Monroe than Mary Pickford, more in Clark Gable than Ramon Navarro. This has nothing to do with any difference between talkies and silent pictures, simply that stars from forty years ago are better remembered than those from sixty or seventy years ago.

New generations of movie memorabilia collectors are likely to seek material connected with Robert Redford, Paul Newman and Clint Eastwood as Bogart, Flynn and others fade into the past.

Old and very new movie memorabilia, from Rambo *to the personal letters of Arthur Askey.*

MUSICAL BOXES

The man who laid the groundwork for the age of the musical box was a Swiss, Antoine Favre, who invented a 'comb' of musical metal teeth for use as chimes in clocks and watches. The real revolution came in 1818 when a manufacturer called David Lecoultre mated a one-piece metal comb with a rotating cylinder studded with hundreds of carefully placed pins. As the cylinder turned, the pins were touched by the pre-tuned teeth in the comb and so a tune was played.

This basic design was used for the next fifty years, until the musical box was made obsolete by the invention of sound recording, but in its heyday the musical box was a sensation.

Large numbers of them, playing popular tunes, or airs, as they were known, were sold. A clockwork motor powered the revolving cylinder and more complicated models could play several different tunes which were usually listed on a decorated card fitted in the inside of the lid.

The boxes themselves were later embellished with inlay, gilting and mother of pearl. Bells, flowers, even moving metal butterflies were added to the interiors. Yet it is ironic that the ones which are most beautiful to look at are these days often the least valuable, for all this decoration and gimmickery indicates in most instances a model of fairly late manufacture and collectors prefer earlier, simpler models. Even so, all cylinder musical boxes are sought after and even the most garish example can fetch several hundred pounds. Early models, particularly by certain makers, can fetch several thousands pounds each.

In 1885 another type of musical box became briefly popular, the polyphon, or symphonium, as it was also known. This utilized a rotating metal disc instead of a cylinder. The advantage of this was that the disc could be made more cheaply and quickly than the cylinders, allowing popular tunes to be marketed more rapidly.

Coin operated models became available eventually and were installed in cafes and inns – a form of juke box. But as the nineteenth century neared its end, the invention of recorded sound by Thomas Edison spelled the demise of most forms of musical box. First the phonograph and then the gramophone took over and a great industry fell into decline.

An example of a Victorian multi-tune musical box.

OIL LAMPS

The place most people associate with the oil boom is Texas, yet ten years before the first well was sunk in America a man called James Young struck it rich drilling for oil in the Scottish Lowlands. The oil he found wasn't present in vast quantities, but there was enough to allow him to develop and patent a refining process in 1850, which gave the world paraffin. The manufacture of the paraffin, or as they are more widely known, oil lamp, soon followed, and they have become synonymous with the Victorian period.

The introduction of the flat, cog-wound wick boosted the industry and when Joseph Hinks invented the Duplex Burner – a two-wick burner which greatly increased luminosity – in 1865, the oil-lamp industry was set for a glowing future. Between 1859 and 1870 about eighty patents *each year* were registered in connection with different oil lamps. The main one was the invention of the circular wick central draught burner which made it possible to have an oil lamp giving an amazing 200 candlepower.

Oil lamps were manufactured on such wide scale that the present-day collector faces a bewildering choice of models spanning a huge price range. Original quality often determines current value. Some humble Victorian oil lamps made for use in working class cottages are still available for £20 or £30, which is less than the price of some reproduction lamps. But high quality models, made for use in wealthy homes, can fetch several hundred pounds. Such lamps often had cut-glass founts, Corinthian pillars and embossed decorative bases and fittings.

If you are contemplating buying an old lamp, there is one thing above all else you must bear in mind. The beautiful glass shades these lamps had have mostly been smashed over the years and the ones for sale in antiques shops or at fairs are usually fitted with a reproduction shade. While this, of course, is preferable to not having a shade at all, a lamp with its original fitment is more desirable and worth paying more to obtain. Unfortunately, to the unskilled eye new and old shades can look very much the same and if you are prepared to pay a good price for an oil lamp, then it is worth questioning the dealer about the authenticity of the shade.

In addition to table oil lamps, there are a large number of other designs, including wall mounted examples, hand lamps, and more unusual examples such as students' reading lamps, which have a gravity-fed reservoir and are very sought after by collectors. There were also oil-powered hanging lamps, standard lamps, swing bracket lamps, and even oil lamps specially designed to be mounted on pianos.

A nineteenth-century oil lamp with a gilt stem and enamelled glass reservoir. The base is made of stone.

PAINTINGS

If you visit an antiques dealer or art specialist, clutching an old painting that has been in the family for many years, you are likely to be very disappointed with the valuation you are given. For most old paintings – oils or water colours – even if the best part of a century old, are likely to be worth comparatively little, simply because they were painted by amateurs.

I am frequently asked how easy – or difficult – it is to determine whether a painting is by a professional artist or was done by a talented amateur. It is a difficult task which usually requires some years of experience to develop an eye for style and quality. That task is not helped by the fact that some of the most talented professional artists painted in a way which looks, to the untrained eye, very amateurish.

Painting in both oils and waters colours has been a popular pastime for at least two centuries. Everyone has painted at some time, even if only with a toyshop paintbox. Those with a liking for it continued well beyond their schooldays and often had sufficient ego to have their work expensively framed. This has meant that the art market is awash with amateur paintings, most of which are worth less than the frames they are in. No matter how good an artist is, he has to have achieved national recognition and probably have exhibited at the Royal Academy or some lesser institution before art dealers and collectors take much notice.

Most Victorian and early twentieth-century paintings are not worth a great deal unless they are by an artist of some repute and who has something of a following among collectors. Of course, not all artists have to have achieved *national* fame. There are many who have attained a regional reputation, confined to, say, Norfolk, or the Lake District, but whose work is still sought after.

Unless your old painting does have that professional touch however, you are very unlikely to be able to retire on the proceeds of its sale. From time to time, paintings do surface from attics or country auctions that when finally sold, perhaps in London at auction, achieve heady prices that make headlines. So you should never entirely abandon hope.

But downscale from these high prices there is a vast quantity of very pleasant paintings available at very little money, mostly between £20 and £50, which have the advantage of being cheap enough for the novice collector – and a very decorative aid to furnishing.

A point worth remembering when collecting paintings is that the frames can sometimes be worth more than the painting.

PAPIER MÂCHÉ

Papier mâché is a French term meaning much as it sounds – mashed paper. It is a form of decorative art first practised in Persia and the East, in France from the middle of the eighteenth century and became popular in England from around 1775.

Papier mâché is composed of a paper pulp prepared from shredded paper mixed with glue or flour and water, with chalk and occasionally sand added. After being pressed, the mixture is moulded and baked. The resulting product is remarkably strong and can be sawn as well as highly polished by a process similar to japanning.

Its strength meant that it could be used to make not only small objects such as snuff boxes, jewellery cases and screens and trays but also small items of furniture such as side tables.

In 1772, Henry Clay of Birmingham devised and patented a variation of papier mâché. Clay's ware, as it became known, was prepared from strong sheets of paper pasted together. By this method, larger items of furniture could be made. This form of papier mâché was popularized in the nineteenth century by the firm of Jennens and Bettridge. Items by this firm, marked with the maker's name or initials on the underside, command high prices.

The colour of finished papier mâché is usually black but red and green base colours were also used. It could and was however, frequently inlaid with mother-of-pearl and further embellished with hand-painted designs and gilding.

Although the material is strong, finished items are vulnerable to chipping and scratching along the edges, and collectors tend to avoid items which have started to look rather shabby. Examples in mint condition can command substantial prices especially for larger items such as tables, chairs, cabinets and work-boxes.

Japanned papier mâché dominated the market during the first half of the nineteenth century. The example at the rear is inlaid with mother-of-pearl, while the case in the forefront is painted in the 'chinoiserie' style.

PARIANWARE

Many people have ornaments made from parian which they greatly treasure, so I suppose I shouldn't really tell them it is often known as 'Poor Man's Marble'. It sounds a rather derogatory term, yet parianware is really of good quality and is often more detailed than its glazed counterparts.

The reason that parianware came into being is an interesting story. In the early 1800s there was a fad for collecting decorative figures and marble was the most popular of materials, though expensive. The Stoke-on-Trent firm of Copeland and Garrett saw the possibility of a lucrative market if they could produce an unglazed porcelain that simulated marble. Parianware was the result of their experiments, and was so named because it resembled marble quarried on the Greek island of Paros.

The new material had very attractive qualities and found an eager market. It had particular use in making figures and the finish was such that they looked like expensive ornaments, yet could be made at low cost. Amazingly, the Copeland firm failed to patent parianware and other firms quickly copied it. Minton, Goss, Royal Worcester, and others made parianware, and even Wedgwood produced a version which they called Carrara, after the famous Italian marble.

Much parianware was exported to America. In 1852 however, the United States Pottery Company at Bennington, Vermont, began producing parianware figures. These can be identified by the name of the company in a ribbon. This ware was particularly noted for its beautiful flower and foliage decoration. Such items are now scarce for the company went out of business in 1858. As a result they are highly collected.

Parianware was later widely produced in Europe, notably in Saxony and Thuringia, and undercut the British ware, forcing British manufacturers to produce different, more profitable lines. Tinted and coloured parianware was popular from around 1870.

Values can vary greatly depending on the subject and size. Smaller examples, just a few inches high, can still be bought for under £50, though larger figures can fetch several hundred pounds if the subject is especially interesting and detailed.

Parianware was also known as 'Statuary Porcelain' and its creation enabled the Victorian middle class to collect scaled-down copies of work by leading sculptors.

PEWTER

Pewter is a rather dull alloy and not at all attractive to many people, but it does have its devotees. It is made of tin with small amounts of lead, copper or antimony added, in order to improve its appearance and durability. The Romans introduced pewter to Britain but it was not until 1348 that a pewterers' company was established in London and monitored manufacture from then on.

The pewterers' company declared that only the first grade of pewter could be used in plates, dishes and similar items. Fine pewter was defined as consisting of tin admixed with brass to the extent of 23 percent. Hollow ware on the other hand, such as tankards and flagons, was decreed to be made from 26 parts of copper to 112 parts of tin; this varied however, according to the shape and purpose of the vessel. Ley, or common pewter, consisted of 80 parts tin to 20 lead, while a variety called 'trifle' consisted of 83 parts tin to 17 parts antimony.

In 1503 a system of compulsory marking was introduced. Unfortunately, in 1666, during the Great Fire of London, Pewterers' Hall was burned down and all its records destroyed. However, the system quickly re-started and all the marks – or touches, as they are known – since then have been recorded, and it is therefore possible to trace which company made a particular article.

Pewter has mainly been used in domestic wares such as candlesticks, tankards, plates and flasks. While much pewter is plain, some decoration, either by cast methods or embossing, was done, along with engraving. Values vary enormously, depending on age and maker, and keen collectors are really only interested in quite early pieces, from the seventeenth and eighteenth centuries.

Two categories of pewter attract high prices – early pewter and Art Nouveau and Art Deco pewter – the latter often manufactured specifically for Liberty under the brand name of 'Tudric'. Pewter for Liberty usually bears a code number on the base prefixed '01'.

From the Jacobean to the Art Deco period, pewter has always been desirable.

PHONOGRAPHS

A little over a hundred years ago sound was recorded for the first time and the result was the widespread manufacture of what came to be known as 'talking machines'. The first such machines were called phonographs and were invented by Thomas Edison.

In 1877 Edison had been working on a device which could record and play back the dots and dashes of morse code. It occurred to him that it might be possible to 'trap' the human voice and he quickly sketched a device which he felt might work and gave it to his engineer to build.

The prototype was a hand-wound machine and when Edison shouted 'hallo' into the horn he did hear a sound when it was played back, although it didn't much resemble 'hallo'. After some modifications which included substituting tinfoil for wax paper to take an impression of the sound he recited 'Mary had a little lamb' into his new machine. On playback the rhyme could be heard, if a little indistinctly. 'I was never so taken aback,' Edison is reported to have said.

Edison had several hundred machines made and, while they were a sensation when they were demonstrated, the sound quality was still poor and they generated little commercial interest. At that time they were seen largely as a scientific instrument rather than a potential form of entertainment. Even so, by the mid-1880s several companies were manufacturing phonographs under licence from Edison and the machines were constantly being refined. By the 1890s the phonograph had developed a strong following in America and Europe after its potential for recording music and singers was realized. However, the phonograph was to have a comparatively short life for at the turn of the century the flat disc gramaphone came into use, cheaper to make and therefore sell, and with a much better quality of sound. By World War I the phonograph was in effect dead.

These machines, which play fragile wax cylinders, do have a devoted following among collectors though prices are already at a level which the beginner will find off-putting. Machines by the Edison company are the most sought after as they were invariably the best quality. The most popular Edison machine was the Gem, the baby of the family. Other Edison models include the Standard, Triumph, Fireside, Home, and Opera. It is the Opera model which is the most scarce and a fine example would cost thousands rather than hundreds of pounds.

There are many other manufacturers of phonographs whose products attract collectors including Columbia, the French firm Pathe, and the German company Puck. None of these companies made machines which were comparable in quality to Edison but they did turn out some unusual, interesting phonographs and it is the more novel examples that are most appealing. For instance, in 1900 the Columbia firm produced a phonograph which had three horns, giving a sort of stereophonic effect. In 1906 the Puck company produced a phonograph with a cast base in the form of a siren-like maiden seated on rocks playing a lyre.

An Edison Standard Phonograph and rolls.

PLAYING CARDS

If you buy a card game such as Snap or Happy Families, it is likely that within a few months one or two cards will get crumpled, torn, or even lost. If the game is played often, then the cards will become soiled and frayed and you will probably have to throw them away. After all, card games are hardly expensive and are easily replaced. And it is for precisely that reason, cards being cheap, throw-away pastimes, that old sets of cards are becoming increasingly valuable in collecting circles, because old complete sets are now quite rare.

While there is a market for ordinary playing cards, such sets do have to be at least nineteenth century, preferably eighteenth century, to have much collecting potential. This is because the design of the normal playing card has not varied much during the last century or more, and it is differences in design that make cards collectable.

The boom in card collecting is not so much for the regular cards as for specialized games such as Snap, Happy Families and the like, where manufacturers use many designs to catch the eye. Take Snap, for instance. This game is as popular as ever, but almost every year manufacturers change the illustrations on the card face, if only in small detail. These differences are fascinating to collectors. Over 50 or 100 years design changes can mirror social patterns, the way people dress and behave.

Around the turn of the century, one manufacturer produced cards depicting famous poets. Another featured politicians, and another Dickens characters. Some card games have had cartoon illustrations; others featured wildlife, while some depicted royalty. All these sets are now highly sought after, but only if complete and in good condition. Prices can be quite staggering, sometimes running to hundreds of pounds in the case of rare sets.

Among the more unusual sets was one called *The London Post*, issued about 1900 and illustrated with famous landmarks in the London postal districts. Another was called *Bread and Honey* and showed kings, queens, birds and clowns. An example of a firm exploiting a famous incident was the game, *The Search for Dr. Livingstone*.

Not all valuable sets are necessarily more than a 100 years old. Early this century the Mazawati Tea Company issued a card game called *Our Kings and Queens* with beautiful illustrations of English monarchs. Although thousands of these were issued, few have survived and would now fetch well over £100.

More recent events can also produce a valuable card game. In 1963 an enterprising firm produced a card game based on the American President John F. Kennedy. Six weeks later Kennedy was assassinated and the game was withdrawn. Yet in that short period thousands of sets were sold and all have become valuable collector's items.

Late nineteenth-century examples of playing cards often abandoned the traditional suits, indicative of the Victorian antipathy towards gambling.

POP MEMORABILIA

Pop memorabilia is a new and rapidly expanding field for collectors, arguably stemming from the tremendous impact on pop music of the Beatles. Certainly it is items relating to the 'Fab Four' which are in the greatest demand, and fetching astonishing prices.

The intense level of interest in items relating to the group's heyday was made all the greater by the untimely killing of group member John Lennon. Items associated with him attract premium prices, with handwritten song lyrics and sketches by him commanding thousands of pounds. There is considerable interest in lesser items associated with the group, even to the cheap souvenirs sold by the million for just a few shillings in the mid-1960s.

Mugs and plates depicting the group, plastic brooches, dolls, even nylon stockings with woven caricature portraits of the group are now in demand. Records by the Beatles have no special value unless they are demonstration discs, or are autographed by the group. Any material signed by the Beatles is collected. Fans who thought they obtained the group's signature during concert tours will be surprised to learn that the autographs were often signed backstage by some of the group's aides. These fake signatures are detectable by experts.

Unofficial photographs of public appearances by the group, taken by fans, are of increasing interest to collectors and these 'snaps' can fetch several hundred pounds if complete with negatives and sold with the copyright. There is also demand for official publicity photographs, posters and other advertising material relating to the group. This has already extended to the group Paul McCartney went on to form, Wings.

Interest in other pop artists is less predictable; letters, photographs and personal possessions of artists such as Elvis Presley, Bill Haley, Buddy Holly and other famous names have come under the auctioneer's hammer from time to time but by and large, prices have been well below the level of items connected with the Beatles. But there are signs that as Beatles' material gets too expensive for keen young pop collectors, they are turning their attention to the group's contemporaries such as the Rolling Stones, Cliff Richard and The Who.

There is also demand for early records by artist such as T Rex and the Sex Pistols, but whether such items have any lasting value remains to be seen.

Mass-produced publicity relating to pop stars, as seen here, is still within a reasonable price range. Their personal effects, however, can be expensive.

POSTCARDS

The postcard may appear to be a rather insignificant item to collect. Yet there are some old postcards worth several hundred pounds each. But before you dive headlong into the sideboard in a feverish search for granny's old holiday cards, I must stress that the vast majority are worth only pence each.

While you may not locate a really rare and valuable example in granny's old album, it is possible you could discover some cards worth several pounds each. The postcard craze began in the 1890s, reached its heights in the Edwardian era and declined after the First World War. But when the boom was at its peak, everyone collected old postcards and put them in albums. The albums would be shown to friends, rather like we show holiday snaps today.

Cards reflected social change and provide collectors with a fascinating insight into the daily life of the country around the turn of the century.

There are two basic types of postcard: the photographic and the artist-drawn. Photographic cards are photographs in postcard form. Collectors have vast fields to choose from. General landscapes or views tend to be the least valuable, but ones showing people, streetscenes, transport and buildings can be of greater interest and greater value. There is special interest in certain types of card showing, for example, aircraft, motorcars, fire engines, trams, tradesmen, workmen and children.

Cards by artists can be much more valuable. Art Nouveau artists such as Raphael Kirchner and Alphonse Mucha, both of whom drew beautiful, unattainable women, can easily fetch £50 each and often more. Another collected postcard artist, Louis Wain, who specialized in drawing cats, is dealt with separately in this book. The comic seaside postcard is probably the best known of all and Donald McGill and Tom Browne are its most famous exponents. McGill is also dealt with separately in this book.

The rarest and therefore the most valuable postcard is said to be the one issued in 1903 as a fund-raising card for Lifeboat Saturday. It depicts a large hot air balloon. The reason the card is so sought after collectors will pay several hundred pounds for a mint example – is that as a gimmick at the time, the postcards were taken up in a balloon and given a special 'balloon post' postmark while in the air.

The later Victorians were enthusiastic users of postcards, a fashion which grew out of the popularity of photography. Picture postcards were first produced on the Continent.

POT LIDS

These days consumer products are attractively and colourfully packaged to attract the attention of potential customers. But in the last century packaging materials were much more limited and Victorian marketing experts came up with an idea to sell particular products, which has resulted in a collecting trend more than a hundred years later.

At first, goods such as meat pastes, pickles, cosmetics, creams and toothpaste were sold in small, plain-lidded pots, and looked dull and uninteresting. Perhaps inevitably, someone somewhere decided to put pretty pictures on the lids of their pots to attract the attention of customers, and the habit became widespread. These pot lids, mostly about 8 cm (3 in) in diameter, were decorated with beautifully painted scenes. Some were landscapes, others historical figures. Birds, animals, flowers, romantic couples, all appeared on pot lids. At the time, they were hardly collected, yet because they were made in millions, many have survived.

Today their beauty is appreciated. Some examples can be worth more than a hundred pounds. Many firms made these pot lids, but by far the best known is F. and R. Pratt of Stoke-on-Trent. In 1847 Felix Pratt took out a patent which allowed the mass manufacture of decorated pot lids which until then had been made more laboriously. Many lids were such works of art that the artists actually signed them, as with a painting. The most notable artist was Jessie Austin and his work is greatly in demand by collectors.

By the turn of the century the great heyday of the pot lids was over as tin and other materials took over from pottery as the most widely used packaging material. Many pots and lids were kept by families who used them as containers for household items such as pins and buttons.

It is worth noting that pot lids have been widely reproduced and even faked over the years. If it is a collecting field that interests you, it would be wise to ask the seller for a receipt stating that it is a nineteenth-century example.

A selection of pot lids, a field that offers almost unlimited scope to the collector, since manufactured examples run into the thousands.

POTTERY COTTAGES

With property prices steadily rising, it is comforting to know you can still go out and buy a picturesque country cottage for as little as £50. The snag, of course, is that you won't be able to live in it; after all, it will only be about 12 cm (6 in) high.

Pottery cottages and houses were immensely popular ornaments throughout the last century, and while they cost only a shilling or two then, demand for them today is so great that some examples can run to hundreds of pounds.

Mostly made in Staffordshire, these miniature homes can be very charming with decorative details including flowers around the front door. They come in a wide variety of designs, from a humble rustic cottage to a stately home or castle. The best and most valuable examples were made between 1800 and 1850. After the latter date, quality deteriorated.

Most early items have no manufacturer's name, but ones that can be safely attributed to the Pratt Company are in great demand and command very high prices. Lesser makes are valued according to their unusualness; in general the more detail the better the price. Decorations can include flowers, dogs, sheep or human figures.

Not all cottages are purely for ornament. Some were made as money boxes with a coin slot in the roof or at the rear. Others could be used as vases or spill holders. Many were made as pastille burners; a slow-burning, fragrant material could be burnt inside, with the scent drifting out of the chimney.

Collectors pay very good prices for special properties such as the homes of the famous, like Warwick Castle or Balmoral Castle. But even better prices can be obtained for homes of the infamous. Among these is Potash Farm, home of murderer James Rush. He killed the Recorder of Norwich in Victorian times and pottery makers, keen to cash in on his notoriety, made not only models of Rush's house, but of his luckless victim who resided at Stanfield Hall. Potash Farms can be worth up to a couple of hundred pounds.

Another desirable residence, for collectors at least, is the home of Palmer, the Staffordshire poisoner who murdered his wife, brother and several friends in order to claim insurance money to meet gambling debts. Palmer was hanged at Stafford in 1856 and models of his house sold by the thousand.

The Crimean War also figured in pottery buildings, with the fortress at Sebastopol and at Malakoff among military establishments featured. These are fairly rare and can fetch more than £200 each.

Pottery homes tend to attract many novice collectors, particularly at the lower end of the price scale, but a word of warning. These tiny homes have been widely reproduced and faked, and it is best to buy from a reputable source.

Staffordshire pottery cottages have a naive charm. The example on the left was used as a pastille burner.

PRINTS

When a drawing or painting is copied onto a metal, wood or stone template and this used to reproduce the original, usually in large numbers, the result is called a print. Pictorial prints were introduced soon after printing itself came into use in the mid-fifteenth century. The earliest prints were done by means of plates of carved wood, though the use of copper plates soon became established.

There are three basic ways of producing a print; the first is the relief process in which the surface to be coated with ink stands proud from the plate itself. The second, the intaglio process involves the design being cut into a thin metal plate, which is then inked and wiped, leaving the incised area filled with ink. The printing then takes place under pressure which forces the paper into the incisions. Included in this process are both line engraving and etching. The third process for making prints is called planographic of which lithography is the main technique. In this process designs are drawn onto stone or alloy plates, using a greasy crayon. The surface is then washed with water and rolled with a greasy ink; the wet surface repels the ink which adheres only to the areas drawn with greasy chalk.

Prints vary enormously in price depending upon who produced them, and what they depict. Until the invention of photography in the mid-nineteenth century, prints were widely used to convey information. Thus many show new buildings, prominent people, fashions, animals and beauty spots such as the Lake District. Among collectors, sporting prints are popular as too are prints relating to transport, railways, canals and natural history prints.

Some collectors look for works by particular artists rather than for subject matter. Among the best known are William Hogarth whose work frequently had a moralistic message, James Gillray who was a noted caricaturist, and Thomas Rowlandson whose best-known work is satirical. Identifying and dating prints can often be quite simple as many examples bear the name of the artist and engraver and the date of publication in small print along the foot of the picture.

Prints from the seventeenth and eighteenth centuries can command good prices but there is a wealth of nineteenth century prints available for very little money. In particulab, Victorian prints were produced in such great numbers that general price levels are quite low, but even this era has its notables, among them the colour prints of George Baxter and Abraham La Blond.

Also eagerly collected are Pears prints, issued by the famous soap company between 1891 and 1922. The firm's marketing boss, Thomas Barratt, felt that prints would not only be an excellent form of advertising, but would provide a 'poor man's picture gallery'. More than 100 different titles were published, and their charm and appeal have proved so enduring that they are still reproduced in large numbers today, both as posters, and on birthday cards.

Large, original Pears prints now fetch £50 or more, but as the market is flooded with copies, it is wise to seek a guarantee of authenticity.

A pleasing example of a print issued by the Pears soap company.

RADIO

How many of you, I wonder, remember those primitive radios called crystal sets, with their tuning devices, or 'cat's whiskers'. They were first produced in the 1920s and cost only a few shillings.

Not surprisingly, radio caught on fast; from the crackly sound of those crystal sets heard through headphones, the medium moved on rapidly to more elaborate and more sophisticated sets. Within ten years most homes had a radio and the variety on sale in the 1930s was bewildering. While many were table-top size, the demand was really for more substantial radios, usually made as a piece of furniture. But after the war, as the electronics industry developed rapidly, radios became smaller; wood was being replaced by plastics and by the 1950s we were into the age of the transistor radio.

Of course, few things are more useless than an obsolete radio. They became too expensive to repair, so when they broke down they were often thrown away. The result has been a dearth of early radio equipment and now collectors are clamouring for what is left. At antiques shops and fairs all over the country the old radio is beginning to be displayed along with the Victorian vases and Georgian silver.

Some bear such exotic names as Atwater Kent, Somerset-Mars, Gecophone, and Metropolitan-Vickers, recalling the great days of radio manufacturing. And what about the Fellophone Little Giant, proudly bearing the label, 'Entirely British manufacture'.

Vintage radio is a complex world of rheostats, condensers, loading coils and other terms only the true enthusiast can really understand. Some early or unusual radios can be worth hundreds of pounds to collectors. However, there are many available at less than £50. Radios must be pre-war for collectors to be really interested, and models made by commercial manufacturing companies are more sought after than the many home-built models which came in kit form.

Even if old radio equipment is not functioning, and this is likely to be the case, collectors are still interested. They can usually get them back to working order, using spare parts from scrap sets.

Left a Revophone crystal set. Right An Eddystone radio with Amplion horn.

RAILWAY COLLECTABLES

The lure of steam trains is one of the strongest manifestations of nostalgia and there is a growing army of rail enthusiasts who like to decorate their homes with relics from the great age of steam locomotives. They collect not just bits of trains, they collect bits of stations, too. In fact, they collect anything remotely connected with railways.

The railway age began in 1825 with the opening of the Stockton and Darlington line, the first railway to be worked by steam. The rail system developed quickly and that progress continued right up until the death of the steam train in the early 1960s. The collecting age began once the rail system was nationalized, after the last war. It began to boom in the 1960s and 70s and now has a devoted following.

There is an eager market for old railway lamps, signalling equipment, ticket collectors' badges, guards' uniforms, railway timetables, calendars and advertisements, railway notices, crockery, clocks, benches and posters. A locomotive nameplate like Cardiff Castle or King George V will fetch several thousand pounds. But there are many much smaller, and much cheaper, items to be found.

Collectors are particularly keen on railway paraphernalia which contains the name of a pre-nationalization railway network, such as the Great Western, the North Eastern, or the London Midland Scottish. Railway clocks, lamps and small enamelled or cast-iron notices are among the most common items, but still eagerly sought after, while even a set of brass coat buttons bearing railway insignia will have some value.

The most expensive class of rail relic is the engine name-plate, but obsolete station signs, lamps and uniforms such as these are all very collectable.

SAMPLERS

I once heard an antiques dealer trying to describe a sampler to someone who had never heard the term. 'It's a sort of embroidery which is more interesting than ordinary embroidery,' he said. That is hardly an accurate description but I certainly knew what he meant.

Samplers can be fascinating items often taking the form of a stitchwork family document. They are made from pieces of linen embroidered with designs but what sets them apart from other forms of embroidery is that samplers were initially used for instructional purposes, a way of teaching young girls the art of needlework. Consequently samplers are very personal items usually containing the name, age and sometimes a few other details of the person who constructed it. Some of them are remarkably artistic and finely executed considering they were a learning piece.

The earliest reference to samplers dates back to 1502 and the earliest English example to survive is dated 1598. It was made by Jane Bostocke and is kept by the Victoria and Albert Museum. The vast majority of eighteenth-century samplers are records of the maker's ability with a needle. Letters of the alphabet, numbers, borders and small designs such as flowers and animals were the main content though some contain long extracts from religious texts which may have taken months or even years to complete.

The nineteenth century saw a gradual decline in the standards of needlework as changing social patterns provided more things for women to do with their time. There was still great interest in making samplers particularly in the Victorian period but by now they were mostly being done merely as ornamental samplers to be framed and hung on the wall like a picture. The degree of skill and imagination for these works was more limited as by this time sampler patterns were being published which merely had to be copied.

While eighteenth century examples are scarce and can fetch several hundred pounds each, there are still many fine Victorian samplers available at much more modest sums.

Early nineteenth-century samplers by children. The centre example is by one Elizabeth Allison Elland, aged 11.

SCENT BOTTLES

There are some people – mostly men – who would argue that scent is the best example of the diminishing return on an investment. A sum is expended, the product wafts on the air for a few hours and then vanishes entirely, leaving no trace of its presence, and the purchaser considerably poorer. This is a rather cynical view for perfume does perform a valuable role, pleasing both those who use it and those around them. But while cynics might criticize scent they certainly couldn't criticize the scent bottle. Not only is it a thing of beauty but it has proved over the years to be an excellent investment.

Containers for scented water have existed as far back as Roman times and probably much further, but it was not really until the eighteenth century that scent bottles became something of an art form in their own right. Perfume manufacturers realised that the packaging often sold their product and it was important for their sales that their fragrances were available in decorative, eye-catching containers. Many perfume makers actually commissioned designers and craftsmen to construct special bottles for new perfumes and this practice continues to the present day.

While glass has been the principal material used for scent bottles, it is by no means the only one. Both porcelain and enamel were also widely used. The French and the Italians have lead the way in scent bottle design though Britain has made its own contribution. Coloured, cut and engraved glass was used extensively and additional decoration included painting, enamelling, or the use of gold and silver tops and mounts.

Towards the end of the eighteenth century there was a fashion for porcelain scent bottles and such notable manufacturers as the Chelsea factory were making pretty, stylish examples. Those that have survived are now beyond the means of the average collector. Yet there is plenty of scope for a scent bottle collection if Victorian and early twentieth-century examples are sought. They still turn up in quite large numbers at antiques fairs and in shops and, while pricing is linked as much to unusuality as age, plain but still attractive types can cost just a few pounds. In particular it is worth looking out for 1930s Art Deco examples.

Victorian and Edwardian scent and spray bottles. Examples made by individual perfumiers are often valuable.

SCIENTIFIC INSTRUMENTS

A century or more ago, when science was still rather inexact, a wide variety of now obsolete instruments were in use. These instruments, used by surveyors, architects, doctors, dentists and those engaged in many forms of scientific research, were works of the utmost craftsmanship. Often made of brass and housed in lined mahogany cases, beautifully engraved with the maker's name and address, the instruments are now eagerly sought by collectors, who are often still connected with some of the professions mentioned. Surveyors can go into raptures over an eighteenth-century theodolite; dentists just love to get their teeth into early tooth-pulling equipment.

To the layman, most scientific instruments are a mystery. Few of us would know a pantograph from a planimeter, but there is still a ready market for them. Collectors seek microscopes, telescopes, surveyors' levels, compasses, sextants, barometers, drawing instruments, scales and balances, barographs, measuring devices, calculators, and less recognizable items such as telemeters, eidographs, spectrometers and clinometers.

Condition, completeness and rarity decide the value, and makers' names are very important. Among the most collected are instruments by Zeiss, Leitz, Beck, Dolland, Ross, Swift, Troughton and Simms, Nairn, Stodart, and Neal. There are, of course, many others.

An aneroid barometer (foreground), microscope and compass.

SEASIDEWARE

Thinking of summer holidays conjures up in many peoples minds visions of a trip to the seaside. Victorians had just the same outlook and their holiday trips sparked off a souvenir trade which is still going strong today. The take-home trinkets of a hundred years ago are now very popular among collectors, but are so numerous that prices are still low and anyone can afford to start a collection.

The turning point for the souvenir trade was 1871, when the Public Holiday Act became law and gave the working classes guaranteed holidays. That, and the rapid growth of railways, enabled almost anyone to get to the coast, and manufacturers were quick to try to cash in on the trend. With cameras as yet only toys for the wealthy, and picture postcards yet to come, a pictorial souvenir was the only way to show friends what your holiday spot looked like.

The most popular souvenir was made of china and was mostly in the form of a cup and saucer or a jug or dish. These items, mostly coloured a garish pink with vivid gold decoration, usually featured a picture of the resort or some notable landmark. Sold at the time for pence, they now fetch a few pounds each. Blackpool was the most popular resort and souvenirs with pictures of the still famous tower and the then famous big wheel are commonplace.

Most seaside holiday spots had their own souvenirs, but even inland towns miles from the sea produced their own range of take-home items for visitors. Often in such places the new town hall, post office or railway station would be on the picture, rather than the pier or the promenade. Such pictures, transferred from a photographic plate, provide a fascinating glimpse of holidaymakers a century ago and have strong social history appeal for collectors. Trams, bathing huts, penny farthing cycles, floor-length dresses and bowler-hatted men, show just how times have changed.

Most of these china souvenirs were made abroad, often in Germany – or Bohemia as it was known – as wages were much lower than in Britain and it was cheaper to import the goods than have them made here. In that respect, times have not changed too much.

If you are looking out for the seaside souvenirs, then the best place to look is inland shops. The items were sold at the seaside to be brought home for family and friends, so they mostly crop up at inland antique shops, fairs and auction rooms. Building up a collection from one favourite resort is preferable in terms of future value, as a one-place collection is likely to be worth much more if you ever decide to part with it.

From the nineteenth century to the 1940s, lustreware mugs, cups and saucers in shell form, as well as local sand-filled souvenirs, were sold to holidaymakers as cheap and objects for the sideboard.

SEWING MACHINES

I can recall a number of occasions when I have been at an antiques fair and watched someone come in carrying an old sewing machine they wish to sell. In some instances they have carried this heavy item a mile or two from their home or heaved it on and off the bus. When, red faced and out of breath, they place it before the antiques dealer and say: 'What will you give me for this?' it is difficult to be blunt and tell them the truth – that it is worth next to nothing.

While old sewing machines are not quite ten a penny, they were manufactured on a vast scale, were well-made and durable, have remained useful and have thus survived in large quantities. Early machines are collected and are valuable, but when collectors use the term 'early' they refer to a machine usually far older than the one granny had.

The first successful sewing machine was patented as long ago as 1830 by a Frenchman who installed a quantity of the machines in a Paris shop and used them to make army uniforms. However, other tailors thought the invention was such a threat to their livelihood that they broke into the shop and smashed the machines. Of course this did not halt the progress of the sewing machine, which continued to develop quickly throughout the 1830s and 40s.

Many refinements were introduced by manufacturers in a variety of countries, though none of the machines were totally reliable. It was in 1850 that the race to make a perfect sewing machine attracted a man whose name was to become the most famous of them all. That man was Isaac Singer. He saw a sewing machine being repaired in a shop, thought the design very clumsy, and decided to improve it.

In 1851 he patented the machine and within ten years was producing a light-weight domestic machine which worked well and proved popular. Because sewing machines were expensive the Singer company introduced a hire purchase system to sell them and gradually the company became the best known sewing machine manufacturer in the world.

However, keen collectors are really only interested in Singer's first model dating from the early 1860s. A good example could fetch several hundred pounds. By and large collectors prefer more unusual models by lesser known manufacturers, and names to look out for include Cookson, Dolphin, Newton Wilson, White Gem, Howe and Grover & Baker. The more unusual the machine the more likely it is to attract collectors and some models were most unusual. One company, Kimball & Morton, produced one in the form of a lion while another firm produced a delightful machine in the shape of two cherubs, one of whom held the cotton reel spindle in the upright position.

There is demand, too, for toy sewing machines which, though made as play things, usually worked in much the same way as a larger machine. The keenest demand exists for machines made before 1880 and most of these machines did not have a wooden base or a lid.

An early Jones Hand Machine c. 1880.

SILVER

In 1983 an old silver spoon found by a farmer fetched £13,000 when sold at auction and the news headlines that resulted prompted many people to search through their own cutlery in the hope of finding a similar treasure. This particular spoon was hallmarked 1380 and was one of the earliest items of this kind ever found, hence its high value.

The chances of anyone else coming across a silver spoon worth thousands of pounds are remote, but there is no doubt that silver, and cutlery in particular, causes more problems than most in collecting circles. The reason is simply that few people can distinguish a silver hallmark from the many other manufacturers' marks which appeared on silver-plated items. A silver hallmark, or assay mark, is given to silver items of a particular quality – usually around 95 percent pure silver. The designation 'sterling silver' applies to items containing slightly less pure silver.

Foreign silver is mostly of a lesser quality than British, while silver plate, or Sheffield plate, as it is sometimes known, contains merely a thin coat of silver on a copper or metal base. Manufacturers of all these wares have over the years used a variety of tiny symbols, most of which are meaningless to all but the expert. Thus confusion has arisen, leading to many thinking that they own a piece of silver, when in fact they merely have an item of silver plate.

Silver is a metal which is too soft to withstand normal wear and tear, so it is mixed with small portions of other metals, mainly copper, to make a stronger alloy. Obviously, this is a clear field for fraud, so a hallmarking system was devised as long ago as 1300. A silver hallmark is usually made up of three or four symbols set in tiny shields. The important one to look for is the lion. The lion emblem is the official silver assay mark and can be used only on high quality silver. The other symbols on silver denote the town of assay, and the year the item was hallmarked. If a fourth symbol is present, it usually contains the maker's initials.

Various towns were assay centres and have their own symbol. For instance, London has a lion's head, Birmingham an anchor. By checking the symbols in Bradbury's Hallmarking Guide, a small reference book available from most bookshops, silver collectors can date an item to a particular year. This precise dating makes silver collecting quite fascinating, because other collectors can often only guess the date of furniture, brassware, porcelain and other collectables. Careful examination of the symbols, especially on cutlery, is essential because silver plating marks can look like hallmarks to the untrained eye.

Silver is primarily valued by weight, which supplies a basic scrap value, and that price is then increased when related to age, condition, and degree of decoration.

Examples of Victorian and Edwardian silverware. You might start your collection by, say, specializing in salt spoons or ornamental sugar tongs.

SMOKERS' REQUISITES

Smoking is regarded as one of the worst habits known to man, but in addition to the millions addicted to tobacco, there are a growing number of people addicted to collecting smoking memorabilia, which is not so lethal, and certainly more interesting.

Old pipes, cigarette cases, cigar boxes, tobacconists' signs, cigar cutters, smoking cabinets, tobacco jars, cigarette holders and vesta cases provide the smoking afficionado with a vast choice of collecting themes.

Pipes have always been popular with collectors and the most sought after is the Meerschaum, made from a soft white clay found mainly in Turkey and often modelled into human and animal forms. These pipes were so popular in Victorian times that one-upmanship was measured by how discoloured the pipe bowl became. When smoked, a Meerschaum changes from white to lovely hues of honey, amber and brown. Elegant young gentlemen 'breaking in' a new Meerschaum would often pay a young lad to smoke their pipes virtually round the clock to hasten the discolouring process.

These days, a fine Meerschaum can fetch several hundred pounds, depending on its design.

Although smoking has been a male habit for hundreds of years, it was not socially acceptable for woman until about the turn of the century and even then, women preferred to smoke cigarettes using a holder. These were often made from silver and tortoiseshell. Some were made with gold mounts, some were carved with relief decoration, and most came in a small leather case. They are much collected these days.

During the nineteenth century matches were not carried in boxes, but in vesta cases, silver or silver plated and decorated with embossing or engraving. These are dealt with separately in this book.

Cigar and cigarette boxes often came in novelty designs, sometimes having musical movements or trick mechanisms revealing secret compartments. Even as late as the 1930s, novelty boxes like these were still popular.

Collecting any kind of smoking memorabilia has one distinct advantage – at least your investment won't be going up in smoke.

Smoking accessories. At the rear is a smoker's cabinet containing a tobacco jar.

SNUFF BOXES

Snuff is actually powdered tobacco and it has been used for many centuries. Most people seem to regard it as a rather filthy habit and even those that don't look on those who perpetrate it as rather eccentric. Snuff-taking seems to have become established in Europe in the sixteenth century and by the end of the eighteenth century had become a rather fashionable habit in the higher levels of society.

Snuff boxes from this period were often made in gold and elaborately decorated with embossing, enamelling and even by being studded with jewels. Such heady examples are of rather academic interest to the collector these days as the prices they command put them beyond the pockets of all but the wealthy. However, snuff taking continued throughout the nineteenth century and, while it lost popularity among the nobility and gentry, it was an increasingly common practice among the working classes. Consequently there are many snuff boxes still available made from much more humble materials than gold and silver.

Wood, bone, brass, steel and papier mâché were widely used and these can still be acquired quite cheaply. Yet even in catering for this more basic market manufacturers still managed to come up with some very pleasing designs. Papier mâché snuff boxes, for instance, though mostly black in colour normally had beautifully decorated lids with designs in mother of pearl. Snuff boxes made from bone and wood were often carved and even cheap, metal snuff boxes might feature engraved or embossed patterning, so there is plenty of scope to build up a collection at comparatively low cost.

Victorian snuff boxes, including an interesting example in tortoiseshell.

STAFFORDSHIRE FIGURES

Many people consider Staffordshire figures to be the most crudely made and least appealing of all the pottery produced in the latter half of the nineteenth century. Yet those who collect these flatback figures consider them to be most attractive. Certainly they have a quaint charm which is almost as odds with their lowly origins.

Flatback figures were very popular early in the Victorian period when it was fashionable among the masses to display ornaments on mantle-pieces. Manufacturers did their utmost to encourage the fashion as it was possible to make the figures at very little cost. It was necessary to mould and decorate only the front of the figure, leaving the back smooth and white.

The range of figures was immense and included young lovers, animals, public figures and historical characters. Queen Victoria herself was depicted in flatback form along with a number of other members of the royal family, and these regal examples are among those most keenly collected. But in rather stark contrast, Victorian manufacturers also made figures in the form of well known thieves and murderers, among them highwaymen Dick Turpin. There were explorers and politicians featured along with bare-fist fighters and military leaders.

Perhaps not surprisingly, in the days when women were down-trodden, very few flatbacks were made of notable females, though singer Jenny Lind and nurse Florence Nightingale achieved this rather dubious honour. Many figures utilized trees and flowers as background decoration and are inevitably prone to damage over the years. Good examples which have remained intact can now command several hundred pounds each but it should be pointed out that Staffordshire figures are among the most reproduced and faked of all pottery. While copies generally tend to have a more shiny glaze and stronger colouring, many have been deliberately aged by greedy dealers who can duplicate the cracks and grime of a 100 years almost overnight, using chemicals and high-baking techniques.

When buying any Staffordshire figure it would be prudent to insist on a signed written receipt guaranteeing the authenticity.

Typical examples of Staffordshire flatbacks. Kilted Highlanders as well as milkmaids were particularly popular in the latter half of the nineteenth century.

STEREOSCOPES

Those who think that the 'stereo' is a modern invention will be surprised to learn that the Victorians had stereo. But not stereo sound, stereo vision.

As early as the 1860s, not all that long after the birth of photography, the stereoscope was in popular use. It was a 3D effect, achieved by two identical photographs being pasted side by side on a card and then examined through a special viewer. The effect of 3D on Victorian society was nothing short of spectacular. People clamoured to buy viewers to take part in the great craze. In order to meed demand for sets of cards showing different scenes, photographers scoured the world to take new and exciting views. Egypt, The Alps, Paris, the African jungle, all were brought before eager eyes anxious to see faraway places in fabulous stereo vision.

Manufacturers created a variety of stereoscopic viewers ranging in quality from flimsy to lavish. Basic models were hand-held, with a sliding facility for focussing. These days such examples are fairly common in the antiques trade and fetch around £25, but the real demand from collectors now is for the more elaborate models, some of which are worth several hundred pounds.

Often made in quality wood such as walnut, rosewood and mahogany, they were craftsman built and many have survived the passing years in near pristine condition. Table models come in two basic types: one is the hand-focussed viewer which accepts one card at a time; the other has a more complicated multicard facility which takes a complete set of cards and shows them in order.

The craze for stereoscopes died out in the late Victorian period, but revived briefly around the turn of the century.

A late-Victorian stereoscope. While not always easy to find, the cards often turn up at sales or in junk shops.

STUFFED ANIMALS AND BIRDS

I once rang a friend of mine, an auctioneer, and he was rather breathless when he answered the telephone. When I learned the reason for his puffing and panting, I was hardly surprised. 'I have a ten-foot tall, stuffed elephant jammed in the saleroom door,' he told me between gasps. Apparently, the creature was defying the efforts of my friend and half a dozen porters to force it through the door.

A stuffed elephant is probably the ultimate challenge for a taxidermist, though large animals were commonly preserved in this way a century ago.

The art of taxidermy in primitive forms goes back to around 5,000 BC when the Egyptians were trying to preserve wildlife as well as humans. But it was not really until the middle of the last century that it became fashionable to display stuffed birds and animals. What initiated the trend was the Great Exhibition of 1851, which included a special section on new developments in taxidermy. The new method involved the skins being filled with arsenic paste, which acted as a preservative. Skins were stretched over wire frames and then the exhibit would be placed in a suitably lifelike pose in a glass case. These cases could be quite ornate, incorporating plasterwork, foliage and paintings to create a realistic background.

Taxidermy was at its height in the late Victorian and Edwardian periods, but it died out soon after the First World War. It is still practised today, of course, but in minimal form. These days the costs are too high and many species are protected. This means that those who wish to acquire stuffed animals and birds mostly have to look to Victorian examples.

Birds of prey such as hawks, kestrels, falcons and owls tend to be the most sought after and the most valuable examples. The pose of the creature is also important. A bird with outstretched wings is likely to look better, and therefore cost more, than one with is wings closed. Foxes, squirrels, otters, and, of course fish, were also preserved and mounted and are now in demand.

Prices vary greatly, depending on stance and condition. But you are unlikely to acquire a nicely-posed bird of prey, for instance, for under £100. Larger birds and animals can cost much more. If possible, it is preferable to buy creatures which are mounted in glass cases, because this helps to preserve them and stops dust and atmospheric conditions affecting the fur or feathers. And always try to ensure that you are buying an old exhibit, otherwise you might encourage 'rogue' taxidermists who hunt and kill protected species. A reputable taxidermist will certainly have some 'new' examples, but he will have ensured that they came to him only after dying from natural causes.

Cased, stuffed animals and birds in simulated natural settings are no longer just the hobby of country gentlemen, but they can still command high prices.

TEAPOTS

The cup of tea – symbol of the British way of life – has stirred up a number of collecting trends, but top of the list comes the teapot itself and some of the designs reflect British eccentricity at its most bizarre. While tea drinking started in this country soon after 1600, the great heyday of teapot design was during the Victorian era, as well as the period between World War I and World War II.

It was Queen Elizabeth I who made the initial move to try to bring tea drinking to Britain. She had heard of the Chinese custom of drinking tea and in 1596 she sent three ships to China to bring back some tea. Unfortunately, they were never heard of again. It was another twenty years before tea arrived in Britain – from Holland, which was importing it from Japan. For the first 100 years, tea was drunk without milk and it was not until the early years of Queen Victoria's reign in the 1840s that it became the drink of the masses.

Early teapots are mostly of traditional Chinese shape and decoration, but once the popularity of the drink became widespread, so teapot design became more unusual. Victorian examples are often in the shape of houses, animals, vegetables, even people. Leading public figures of the day – Gladstone, Oscar Wilde, even Victoria herself – were depicted and are greatly sought by collectors.

Prices can vary considerably depending on rarity and makers, but a few interesting Victorian teapots are still on sale at around £25, with examples of extreme designs fetching much more. But the real period for eccentric design was the 1920s and 30s, when teapots were made in the form of racing cars, nursery rhyme characters, aeroplanes, trains, and even an Indian teepee.

Many of these novelty teapots were made by the firm of Sadlers in Stoke-on-Trent. The company did an interesting range of character teapots, including Humpty Dumpty, The Old Woman Who Lived In A Shoe, and Mary Had A Little Lamb. Another popular teapot was the wartime tank, which featured the head of a cheeky British Tommy as the lid. In the 1920s the obsession with the world land speed record was reflected in a racing car teapot, with the numberplate OKT 42. Examples are now fetching £40 to £70 each, though the model is not particularly rare. What is rare is the caravan-shaped sugar basin made to go with it. These mostly seem to have been broken over the years and I have yet to come across an example.

A few examples from the immense variety of novelty teapots, mostly manufactured in the first half of this century.

TEDDY BEARS

Toy bears have existed for centuries, but it was not until 1902 that the 'teddy bear' was created. It was in November, 1902 that the American President, Theodore 'Teddy' Roosevelt, was on a hunting trip shooting grizzly bears. When a tiny bear cub came out of the bushes, the President refused to kill it. A cartoonist, Clifford Berryman, who was among journalists on the trip, drew a picture of the President and the bear cub and it was published in the newspapers.

In New York a toymaker called Morris Michtom saw the cartoon and quickly made some toy bears and put them in his shop window. He called them 'Teddy's Bear' after the President, and they quickly sold out. Before making them in greater numbers, Mr Michtom wrote to the President, asking permission to call them teddy bears, and President Roosevelt agreed.

By 1903 in America, and soon after in Britain, teddy bears were becoming best sellers. At about the same time as Morris Michtom was making his teddy bears, the German firm of Steiff also started to manufacture toy bears which they introduced at the Leipzig Trade Fair. These bears also became very popular and since then, the teddy bear has established itself as the world's favourite toy, and remains a top seller, even in this age of electronic playthings.

The reason for this enduring popularity, I think, is that the teddy bear is more than just a toy. It takes on the role of friend and companion to both children and adults.

For many years the teddy bear has taken something of a back seat to the doll in collecting terms, but this is no longer the case. Collectors now regard the teddy bear with due importance and this is reflected in the high prices that have been obtained for good examples of 'vintage' teddy bears. A fine Edwardian bear, perhaps 60–90 cm (2–3 ft) tall, and in good condition can now be worth £1,000 or more to a keen collector, and even smaller bears, just a few inches high, can still top £50. But unfortunately, few antiques dealers can tell an old bear from a much loved, but relatively modern example, and consequently, rather silly prices are being asked by the trade for every battered bear they lay their hands on, irrespective of its age.

Early bears had rather pointed noses and a slight hump on their back. From about 1920 the facial features were softened and the bears became rather more chubby. Determining the age of teddy bears can be difficult, with factors like the fabric, the stuffing, and the design of facial features playing an important part.

Early teddy bears can often be recognized by their pointed noses; later versions were frequently chubbier with snub noses.

THIMBLES

The thimble is one of the world's most humble products. Most people regard thimbles as entirely practical objects and few would claim them to be things of beauty. Yet thimbles were often made from silver, sometimes from gold and occasionally encrusted with precious stones. While many thimbles are plain, many more are decorative, and these days old thimbles are eagerly sought by collectors.

The thimble has an interesting history. Its origin goes back many thousands of years. There is evidence that cavemen and women used a form of thimble made from rock or bone and the word 'thimble' is thought to come from an old English word, 'thymel', meaning 'thumbstall'. By the fourteenth century thimbles were made from iron, brass or bronze but wealthy households would have them made in gold and silver with crests or coats-of-arms.

It is unlikely that anyone is going to come across thimbles older than the last century, but even these can be surprisingly valuable. Victorian ladies did a great deal of sewing and embroidery, and manufacture of thimbles reached record levels. Even the cheapest thimbles were often decorated with scrolls, foliage, embossing or engraving. Silver thimbles, complete with tiny hallmarks, were widely made and are especially sought these days. Even routine hallmarked examples can fetch £20 or £30.

Thimbles were often made to be given away as a form of advertising with the brand name prominently displayed. It was not only sewing machine or cotton makers who used the thimble for this; companies such as Hovis, Lipton's Tea, Oxo and even Andrews Liver Salts felt the little thimble could still do a big advertising job. These advertising thimbles can now be worth several pounds each to keen collectors.

While modern sewing machines have virtually ousted the thimble as a practical tool, examples are still made, just for collectors, usually in porcelain or enamel work. Specialist firms are making an amazing range of decorative thimbles, depicting such things as birds, flowers, butterflies, famous people, and even historical events. The birth of Prince William, and even the Falklands Victory are commemorated on thimbles.

A selection of thimbles including two porcelain examples, one carrying the logo of the Jones Sewing Machine company.

TILES

The prim and proper Victorians may not have liked a night on the tiles, but they certainly liked the tiles themselves. Decorative tiles, these days confined to bathrooms and kitchens, were put to much wider use a hundred years ago.

Demand for tiles were so great towards the end of the last century that more than 5,000,000 tiles a year were being produced. The Victorians tiled walls, especially in porchways and halls, they tiled floors and even tiled furniture. Chairs often had a single tile inset in the back for extra decoration; washstands had whole rows of tiles as a splash-guard; and even cupboards and cabinets made use of tiles as a focal point.

Fireplaces had tile decoration, too. Tiles were also used, framed in brass and wood, as teapot stands and framed to hang on walls as unusual pictures. Indeed, it is these portrait tiles which are now the most collected. Slightly larger than the standard square tile, portrait tiles often depicted famous characters such as Queen Victoria or the Prime Minister, Gladstone. But animals, particularly dogs, were also a popular subject.

Many such tiles were made by a number of manufacturers, but ones from the Doulton company in Stoke-on-Trent are probably the most appreciated. Framed portrait tiles can fetch £30 or £40, with rarer examples fetching more. For instance, a set of five portrait tiles by the famous designer, Conrad Dressler, have been sold for £750.

Of course, most collectors go for the more humble household tile and these are still inexpensive and come in an overwhelming variety of designs. Many are by anonymous Staffordshire makers, but the better examples came from companies like Doulton and Minton, and the Shropshire firm of Maw and Co.

Routine Victorian tiles can be commonly found in antique shops for between £3 and £10 each.

A selection of pictorial Victorian tiles and abstract Art Nouveau examples.

TINS

I have heard it said that if you store a cornflakes packet for half a century, it will then appear so quaint that collectors will pay money for it. I'm sure that's true. And because of the disposable nature of packaging, little has survived from years ago. That rarity in itself makes an apparently worthless item have some value. Consequently, old biscuit tins, sweet boxes and other products manufactured in tins large and small are now collected, as they form a record of advertising and marketing from a far-off era.

It was not until the 1860s that food packaging began to become more than just a wrapping or container. Fry's and Cadbury's were pioneers of artful packaging and it is generally accepted that the biscuit makers Huntley and Palmer were the most imaginative. The Reading-based firm saw no limit to the type of boxes in which biscuits could be packed and they produced tins in the shape of ships, farmhouses, globes of the world, prams and even books. Rowntrees were another company whose sweets, especially toffees, came in an amazing variety of tins. And even rather humble products, such as Andrews Liver Salts and the Oxo Cube came in attractive tins and retain quaint fascination in an age of plastic and paper packaging.

The value of such tins depends greatly on condition — tinplate is easily scratched — and on the rarity. Elaborate examples, for instance, are biscuit tins in the shape of ships or houses and can be worth as much as £100 each if in pristine condition.

But there are many tinplate collectables available for as little as 50 pence. Small tins which once contained gramophone needles, pen nibs, snuff, throat pastilles, and boot polish still crop up and are collected. These small examples are still inexpensive, though I dare say the situation isn't going to last too long. But happily, small tins can often be acquired for nothing, for your own house or the home of an elderly relative is a good hunting ground for tins of yesteryear. Elderly aunts and grandmothers are forever keeping old tins 'in case they come in handy'.

Often tins are in use for entirely different purposes such as for storing sewing materials, buttons or pins. Garden sheds and workshops are another productive source. Tins have been used for keeping screws, nails and other useful oddments. One of the items in my own collection is a Huntley and Palmers biscuit tin in the form of a bound set of books. It came my way courtesy of an aunt who had been using it for many years as suitably secure storage — for her will!

Late nineteenth- and early twentieth-century tins. Why not use such tins to hold other collectables.

TOY TRAINS

The nostalgic enthusiasm which has helped create the collecting boom in items associated with old railways, and steam trains in particular, is also reflected in current demand for toy trains. During the last 100 years or so almost all boys have had a toy train and these mechanical wonders have proved fascinating for little girls too. Even with today's craze for electronic toys, the toy train is still a popular present for children and that is likely to remain the case for as long as we have railways in any recognizable forms.

The great age of steam trains is understandably the most popular period for collectors and demand is such that some locomotives, just a few inches long, are already fetching several hundred pounds each, and very rare examples can fetch several thousand pounds each.

In the 1850s, not long after the railway network was established, early toy trains were of the push-along variety, designed to run on the floor, not on rails. It was not until towards the end of the nineteenth century that the train set as we know it today became established.

Three German companies were at the forefront of toy train manufacture — Marklin, Bing and Carette. The best known British manufacturer is undoubtedly the firm of Bassett-Lowke which began making model trains at the turn of the century. The company also formed a link with Bing and Carette.

Price levels of all the early toy trains are now so high as to be beyond the means of the novice collector unless he happens to be rather wealthy. New enthusiasts to toy train collecting are forced to go for more recent examples, such as those made by the famous Hornby Company, though good clockwork examples from this firm are now fetching considerable prices and collectors are having to seek out electric-powered examples by Hornby and other companies.

The collecting of toy trains is now so well-established that it represents a sound investment for the enthusiast.

TREEN

Treen – things made from trees – has always attracted collectors because of the unusual, sometimes bizarre, items that have been made.

Treen covers the vast range of small wooden items used in the household, the dairy, the laundry, and on the farm. It includes craftsmen's tools, items used by vets, chemists, dentists, even by smokers and drinkers. Any small article made from a piece of wood is treenware and though such things have always had their place in the collecting world, they have seldom created much excitement. But while treen is usually unspectacular, there is an honest, homely quality about such items which attracts a large number of devotees.

Many collect treen on a particular theme. Kitchen items, for instance, strainers, and butter moulds. From a bedroom there are wigstands, glove stretchers, lace presses, back scratchers and foot warmers. From the laundry, washing bats and from the nursery, moneyboxes, toys, games and miniature furniture.

Agricultural equipment includes sickles, bird scarers, hop clogs, while veterinary instruments include tail dockers, and even pill injectors for forcing tablets down the throat of an animal. Craftsmen's tools are represented in treenware in the form of plumbers' dibbers, masons' mallets, shoemakers' measures, artists' palettes, woodworkers' planes, and even lacemakers' lamps. And among the many other examples are policemen's truncheons, wooden love tokens, especially spoons, and the many small, decorative household ornaments that were carved from wood.

Treenware is something of an acquired taste and this has helped to keep prices comparatively low.

Examples of treen, including a turned-wood tobacco bowl, inlaid serviette rings, and a mosaic playing card box.

TUNBRIDGE WARE

Tunbridge Ware is the name given to mosaic work in wood. This intricate form of carpentry has been well known for at least three centuries but it reached its peak of skill and popularity in the middle of the nineteenth century.

It seems unlikely that the work originated in Tunbridge in Kent though that town did become the centre of the industry, probably due to its long tradition of producing craftsmen who were noted for their wood-working talents. Tunbridge Ware is made with the use of thin rods of wood which are usually dyed different colours then stuck together to a solid block. From this block thin veneers are made which are then used to add decoration to other wooden objects, usually the lids of boxes. Designs were not limited to merely patterned strips but often complete pictures were made up to form very attractive centre panels.

Early examples of the ware were usually platters and small picture frames with simple geometric mosaic patterns. By the middle of the eighteenth century, however, the craftsmen of Tunbridge were applying bands of mosaic to the sides and lids of snuff boxes, trinket boxes, patch boxes, napkin rings and eggcups. Later, in the mid-nineteenth century when elaborate pictures were being composed, a popular subject was a profile of Queen Victoria, particularly on stamp boxes. The profile was based on stamps of the period.

The popularity of Tunbridge Ware grew rapidly in the late Regency and early Victorian periods probably due to Tunbridge Wells itself being a spa town frequented by royalty. There was strong demand for souvenirs by tourists and Tunbridge Ware made the perfect take-home present. Sadly, as it became more and more popular its quality declined and by the end of the Victorian era the industry had died. Although the best examples seem to date from the 1850s and 60s, all types of Tunbridge Ware are collected today and the craft mostly appears on writing boxes and jewellery cases.

Tunbridge ware trinket boxes from the mid-nineteenth century, using complex inlays of colourful foreign woods rather than dyed timber.

TYPEWRITERS

When an antiques dealer sees someone lugging an old typewriter into his shop, his heart usually sinks. Many people believe that just because a typewriter may be fifty or more years old it must be a collectable and therefore valuable. Such people are very reluctant to accept that this is not the case.

Of course, typewriters are collected, but the machines that are most eagerly sought after and have the most value are quite early models dating back 100 years or so, or models by little known or short-lived manufacturers. The typewriter took more than 150 years to evolve, from unsuccessful attempts at manufacturing a writing machine in the early part of the eighteenth century to the first really viable model in America in 1873. Two men, Christopher Sholes and Carlos Glidden, produced the first workable model and its manufacture was taken over by the famous American Remington Company, best known for making guns.

The typewriter quickly caught on and many manufacturers tried to make alternative models using widely differing mechanisms and keyboard layouts. It is such obscure makes, often rather eccentric in design, which greatly appeal to collectors and which are therefore more valuable. Popular models which were mass manufactured are of little interest to the typewriter buff because they are still commonplace.

Clearly most enthusiasts would like to get their hands on one of the early Sholes and Glidden models which would command £1,000 plus from a true typewriter aficionado, but there are many other makes which, in good condition, can fetch several hundred pounds. They include names like the Caligraph, Merritt, Odell, Crandall and Lambert. Well known names such as Underwood, Royal and Smith are of little or no interest.

A 1920s Bar-let typewriter, popular in government departments and the police force.

VESTA CASES

The vesta case is another way of describing a match box. The first friction match was invented by a chemist called John Walker from Stockton-on-Tees but he never patented his discovery and other manufacturers soon began producing their own varieties.

These early matches gave off such a noxious gas that some manufacturers actually printed a warning on the lids of the boxes. There were also severe health risks to those who actually made the matches and strangely enough it was the Salvation Army which stepped in and began to experiment with the use of red phosphorus, a much safer material. Even so, this new brand of matches could still ignite all too easily and needed to be kept in special containers. There was consequently a great demand for vesta cases and manufacturers began turning out masses of both plain and highly decorative examples made in a wide variety of different materials.

As matches were quite expensive, about two pence each in the middle of the last century, those who could afford them could also afford to pay for quite elaborate containers in which to keep them. Pewter, brass and silver were extensively used and often enhanced by embossing, engraving or enamelling. Many of these vesta cases were manufactured with a small ring allowing them to be clipped to a gentleman's watch chain.

Although the kind of saftey match used today was invented in Sweden as far back as 1855, the demand for vesta cases continued until the early years of this century, finally ending at the outbreak of the First World War. Since then matches have been sold in small wooden or cardboard boxes designed to be thrown away.

Collecting vesta cases is a popular hobby for many, largely due to the endless varieties available, their relative cheapness and the fact that a collection can take up so little space. There are many routine examples available at antique fairs for £5 or sometimes less, though hall-marked silver and highly decorative examples command much higher prices. What tends to interest collectors even more are novelty types. These can often be in unusual forms such as faces or animals or have a secondary purpose, perhaps having an additional container for sovereigns, stamps or even for snuff. Some vesta cases, designed to be sold cheaply or even given away, contained advertising messages and these are of special interest to collectors.

Victorian and Edwardian silver and silverplate vesta cases. The inlaid example is a souvenir from a football match at Wembley, 1925.

LOUIS WAIN

Louis Wain was one of Britain's best loved and most prolific illustrators and he should have died a wealthy and happy man. Tragically he died impoverished and insane, but leaving behind a wealth of work which will forever stand as a testament to his talent.

Wain's career as an artist began in the late Victorian era and his gift for drawing, especially animals, quickly made him popular by the turn of the century and up until the First World War. It was almost impossible to pick up a magazine without seeing a Wain illustration on the cover or inside. His drawings were used on calendars, posters, in books and of course on postcards.

He worked for more than thirty British postcard manufacturers as well as some on the Continent. His speciality was drawing cats, usually in human situations, and he tapped a rich vein of humour, using cats to parody human behaviour in a gentle way. Unfortunately as he grew older Wain began to suffer from mental illness and inevitably this began to affect his work.

Those who have made a close study of Wain's drawings claim they can get some idea of his mental condition from the way he drew his cats. They say that when he was sane his cats were lovable and friendly but when he was mad, they took on a menacing, devilish quality.

Wain, like so many artists seemed to have all his talent tied up in his creativity, and he lacked any business acumen. Usually he sold his illustrations for a flat fee which included the copyright, so when his illness was so severe he could no longer work, he had no savings to sustain him and he was taken to the paupers' ward of a London asylum in 1923. He stayed there for two years, until a report in The Times revealed his plight and a public appeal was launched to raise cash to help him. There was a generous response that allowed him to be transferred to a private hospital where he remained until his death in 1939 at the age of 79.

Because Wain was such an industrious artist, his postcards are still fairly common and this has helped hold down prices. Even so, it is increasingly difficult to buy examples for under £20 and his earlier cat cards can fetch much more.

Louis Wain's illustrations of cats were an inspiration for many later illustrators of childrens' books.

WALKING STICKS

In gangster movies, bank raiders usually snarl, 'This is a stick-up' and expect to be handed large sums of money. But if you hold up an unusual walking stick before a keen collector, you could extract a wad of five-pound notes with equal ease.

Collectors will pay as much as several hundred pounds for grandad's old walking stick, provided it has an unusual handle, for it is the handle that makes the stick valuable. The art of carving or decorating stick tops reached astonishing heights. Not only were handles carved into animal or human heads, they were made in a variety of materials including horn, porcelain, glass, silver, gold, ivory and bone. In addition to carving and other embellishments, some stick handles were even mechanical. I have one in the form of a bulldog which, when a small button is pushed, enables the dog to open his mouth and wag his tail.

Other unusual examples included drinking sticks, which had a small flask recessed in the handle and shaft. There were even stick handles which doubled as snuff boxes and coin cases. Some sticks were designed to house swords and guns.

Stick collectors seldom have any difficulty walking. They just want the simple pleasure of owning different examples, each of which is an artistic piece of craftsmanship.

The walking stick became an accessory to dress during the reign of King Henry VIII (1509–47). Henry helped make the stick fashionable because he needed to use them due to his suffering from badly ulcerated legs. But it was the eighteenth century that saw the walking stick reach new heights of decorative splendour. The stick became an essential walking-out accessory, not to aid walking, but simply to carry.

The Victorian period saw the stick retaining great popularity and it is mainly examples from this era which are popular with collectors, as they are still available at reasonable prices.

The swordstick is eagerly sought by collectors, though such a weapon is illegal to carry on the streets. The sword blade is from 60–90 cm (2–3 ft) in length and goes down the shaft of the stick, which effectively acts as a scabbard. Most gentlemen carried such a weapon in the last century as a protection against attacks from footpads – these days known as muggers.

A word of warning however, to would-be collectors. Sword-sticks have been widely reproduced in recent years and in my experience, as many as nine out of ten of those offered on sale in the antiques trade are of this variety.

The walking stick retained widespread popularity until the early years of this century and, in fact, around 1900 the famous jeweller, Carl Fabergé, was making walking sticks including one which was set with garnets, opals, coral, sapphires, pearls, amethysts, moonstone and banded with turquoise.

A selection of nineteenth-century walking sticks, some with novelty handles.

WALL CLOCKS

It is indeed ironic that the name of whoever invented the first mechanical time piece is lost in the mists of time. Mechanical clocks may have their origin in the Middle East. It was not until the eleventh century however, that they began to appear in Europe. Clock ownership was restricted at this time to the very wealthy and to scientists but by the fourteenth century large cities had public clocks on display either in churches or on other distinguished buildings.

Wall clocks at this time were weight driven and smaller versions were designed to be hung on a wall to enable the free fall of the weights.

About 1500 the clock spring was introduced and this has remained the chief method of powering clocks although in recent years quartz has taken over. More accurate time-keeping was possible from the mid-seventeenth century onwards thanks to the use of the pendulum which seems to have originated in Holland. By the nineteenth century demand was growing rapidly for cheap clocks and this demand was mostly met by the Germans and the Americans who went in for mass manufacture. It is mostly this type of wall clock that collectors will come across today, for earlier examples are very expensive.

A typical wall clock was spring driven using a German movement in an ornate case complete with turned pillars, a host of finials, and usually topped by a rearing horse or outspread eagle. Some examples were driven by one, two or in extreme cases three brass weights and these are much more desirable and more expensive. The other clock typical of the late Victorian period is the American regulator, mass produced using cheap veneered wood and sent to Britain by the shipload. Many of these clocks were of the 'drop dial' type with a large white dial 25–31 cm (10–12 in) across and the pendulum visible through a small glass door in the body of the clock. Usually these clock cases were heavily inlaid; the movements were cheap and the construction crude but the clocks did look very attractive and this accounts for their popularity today.

The Americans also sent us large quantities of rectangular wall clocks with painted scenes on large glass doors but despite this decoration the clocks were still slablike and ugly and are not so highly sought after.

The early years of this century saw the arrival of the Edwardian wall clock made mostly in rather plain, austere cases and with a large brass pendulum visible through a panelled glass door. These very serviceable clocks are still available for no more than the price of a modern wall clock and are extremely good value.

A mid-Victorian, single-weighted wall clock.

WINE GLASSES

In the sixteenth and early seventeenth centuries the majority of wine glasses were made in Venice. The glass used was rather lightweight and the stems were elaborately moulded. The bowls were usually funnel or bell-shaped and were frequently engraved.

English glasses tended to follow Venetian patterns, but in the late seventeenth century a man called George Ravenscroft revolutionized the glass industry by inventing a much heavier type of glass which contained lead oxide. English glassmakers then began making rather heavier glasses and from about 1730 designs became much more varied, with the previously simple baluster stem decorated with more bulges or 'knops'. The use of air to create bubbles and twists in the stems also became a feature.

While seventeenth- and eighteenth-century wine glasses can fetch substantial sums, either singly or in sets, there are many nineteenth-century examples which are equally attractive and which can be brought for much less. Indeed, some late Victorian and Edwardian wine glasses can still be acquired for no more than the price of a modern set.

A selection of eighteenth-century wine glasses, including ones with air twist stems.

WOODWORKING TOOLS

Wood is such a versatile material that a bewildering variety of tools exist with which to work it. All such tools are collected but planes are easily the most popular. In the eighteenth and nineteenth centuries furniture was far more ornate than it is today, with extensive use of carving, inlay, cross-banding and other forms of ornamentation. Many of these decorative techniques require special tools, and in particular, special planes.

There is far more scope for collecting in this field than one might suspect. For not only were these woodworking tools required by carpenters, cabinetmakers and joiners but there were a host of specialized tools used by associated trades, such as coachbuilders (including wheelwrights) and coopers (barrel-makers).

While most planes were made for smoothing wood there are many, some of them extremely tiny, which were used for making fine grooves, for inlay, and for carving intricate features. Planes from the eighteenth century can command several hundred pounds, especially if they bear a maker's name such as James Cam or Robert Moore, two of the best known manufacturers. But there are many types of later planes still available for modest amounts. They can be found at farm sales, country antique shops and even in grandfather's old tool box.

There is particular interest in planes, or any tools in fact, which was made to perform a special function. Moulding planes, sill planes, rebate planes and plough planes are just some examples. The more unusual a plane looks the more it is likely to be sought after. If it has the benefit of the maker's name, brass fittings or the date carved on it by the original owner, a common practice, then so much the better.

While there is undoubtedly most interest in planes made of wood, planes made from metal also date back several centuries and these also have a collecting appeal. Downscale from planes come a variety of woodworking tools which are of increasing interest and value. They include braces, augers and other drilling devices, with miscellaneous tools such as saws, gauges, chisels, hammers and axes all attracting the collector. Mostly these tools are obtainable for just a few pounds but that is not likely to remain the case for too long.

A selection of woodworking tools in brass, steel and gunmetal.

WRITING ACCESSORIES

Whilst writing has existed in various forms for many centuries, it was not until the spread of literacy in the nineteenth century that it became a widespread skill.

The quill pen was in use until the early part of the nineteenth century when the steel nibbed pen took over. The inventor of the steel pen is not known but manufacture began around 1830. Of course, like the quill, pens needed frequent dipping in ink, and research continued for a means of making a pen that had its own supply of ink. Many attempts to produce 'fountain pens' were made, some more successful than others.

In 1832 Joseph Parker took out a patent for 'certain improvements' in a self filling pen but it was to be some years before the fountain pen as we know it today was perfected. Today, late Victorian and Edwardian fountain pens are sought by collectors, especially those with notable names such as Parker, Swan and Waterman. As a general rule the more expensive and attractive the pen was when new, the more desirable and valuable it is today.

With the introduction of the Penny Post in 1840 and better education, writing became more and more popular and manufacturers were keen to cash in with not only a wide variety of pens but with associated items such as inkstands, inkwells, pen and pencil cases, stationery boxes and writing slopes. Early inkstands in the seventeenth century were known as standishes. Mostly they were made of silver or were silver-plated but later inkstands, largely from the Victorian period came in humbler materials such as wood, brass and papier mâché. Later examples, usually complete with cut-glass ink bottles, can fetch substantial amounts but many more routine examples are still affordable. There is also a collecting market for small travelling inkwells – ink containers in pocket sized non-spillable cases.

Perhaps the most desirable writing accessory is the writing box or slope itself. This is undoubtedly due to it still being so useful. Rectangular writing boxes opened at an angle in order to form a writing slope which was usually leather inset. Underneath the slope was a space for paper and envelopes, and there were usually compartments for stamps, coins and pens. The boxes came complete with their own inkwells.

Writing boxes were usually made of wood (oak, mahogany and walnut were popular), and were often embellished with decoration in brass, bone, mother-of-pearl or with cross-banding and inlay. Fairly plain late Victorian examples can still be acquired for around £50 but a good quality writing box with an attractive exterior and its original fittings is likely to cost several times this amount.

Victorian writing slopes, inkwells and paperknives are still eminently affordable and add grace and period charm to any desk.

PRICE GUIDE

Prices quoted are for typical mid-range examples in good condition. Rare items may command substantially more; worn, incomplete or damaged items substantially less.

Advertising material £5–50
Aldin, Cecil £20–50
Art Deco £10–150
Art Nouveau £20–120
Automata £400–600
Bairnsfather, Bruce £20–40
Banknotes £2–30
Barometers £150–350
Board games £10–25
Books £10–30
Bottles £3–20
Brass and copper £40–100
Bronze £400–600
Button hooks £3–20
Cameras £15–100
Carriage clocks £75–125
Children's books £3–15
Chinese porcelain £30–1000
Cigarette cards £5–50
Cliff, Clarice £250–2000
Clockwork toys £30–500
Coins £1–30
Comics £5–20
Corkscrews £10–100
Coronationware £20–85
Crested china £5–25
Decanters £30–80
Delft £50–70
Dinky toys £8–150

Dolls £40–3,000
Doulton character jugs £30–250
Egg cups £3–10
Enamels £15–50
Etchings £20–50
Fairings £25–50
Fans £5–20
Firemarks £100–300
Fishing tackle £20–40
Glass paperweights £10–75
Glassware £20–60
Gramophones £35–600
Gramophone records 25p–£2
Hatpins £3–20
Horsebrasses £10–30
Irons £5–30
Jelly moulds £10–65
Kitchen collectables £5–50
Lead soldiers £50–100
Longcase clocks £300–600
Magic lanterns £40–100
Maps £5–150
Medals £5–25
McGill, Donald 50p–£5
Mickey Mouse £5–150
Moneyboxes £5–85
Motoring memorabilia £5–50
Mourning jewellery £15–75
Movie memorabilia £5–75
Musical boxes £200–400
Oil lamps £150–250
Paintings £25–75
Papier mâché £15–75
Parian ware £30–60
Pewter £20–40
Phonographs £150–250

Playing cards £3–30
Pop memorabilia £5–200
Postcards 25p–£10
Pot lids £30–70
Pottery cottages £50–200
Prints £50–75
Radio £50–150
Railway collectables £20–75
Samplers £50–250
Sewing machines £25–50
Scent bottles £10–50
Scientific instruments £25–150
Seasideware £5–20
Silver £20–50
Smokers requisites £2–50
Snuff boxes £10–100
Staffordshire figures £50–200
Stereoscopes £20–30
Stuffed animals and birds £50–100
Teapots £25–75
Teddy bears £100–700
Thimbles £2–25
Tiles £5–40
Tins £2–50
Toy trains £50–100
Treen £5–40
Tunbridge Ware £25–100
Typewriters £15–50
Vesta cases £5–30
Wain, Louis £10–30
Walking sticks £30–100
Wall clocks £250–400
Woodworking tools £5–40
Wine glasses £30–200
Writing accessories £5–50

BIBLIOGRAPHY

Atterbury, Paul, ed., *Antiques: An Encyclopaedia of the Decorative Arts*, (Galley Press)
Benedictus, David, *The Antique Collectors Guide* (Macmillan)
Bly, John, *Discovering English Furniture* (Shire)
Godden, Geoffrey, *The Handbook of British Pottery and Porcelain Marks* (Barrie and Jenkins)
Haywood, Charles H., *Antique or Fake?* (Bell and Hyman)
Mackay, James, *An Encyclopaedia of Small Antiques* (Bracken)
The Lyle Official Antiques Review (Lyle Publications)
Millers Antiques Price Guide (MJM Publications)
The Price Guide To Collectable Antiques (Antique Collectors Club)